Total Archery
Inside the Archer

———

KiSik Lee
Tyler Benner

Astra Archery

Photography:

Bradford Benner (cover photography), Andy MacDonald, Dean Alberga, KiSik Lee, Rick Kramer, two story building, Lars Moeller, Jason Foong, Tyler Martin, Guy Kreuger, and Tyler Benner

A special thank you to all the photographed archers:

Kate Anderson, Tyler Benner, Forrest Blakely, Kristin Braun, Megan Carter, Barbie Cyin, Tyler Domenech, Brady Ellison, Jason Foong, Jake Kaminski, Heather Koehl, KiSik Lee, Khatuna Lorig, Sagar Mistry, Lindsay Pian, Amanda Purvis, Karen Scavotto, Tyler Schardt, Dan Schuller, Lee Stewart, Jacob Wukie, Vic Wunderle, and Nathan Yamaguchi

The sincerest of thanks must be extended to the following people, for without their input, guidance, thought, time, love, support, and belief, this book would not have happened:

Spencer Adamson, Anita Benner, Barbara Benner, Bradford Benner, Ryan Berber, JB Brubaker, Jordan Crumley, Chris Davis, Tony Di Zinno, Sagar Mistry, Josh Pinkerton, Bob Romero, Paul Soady, Thure Stedt, and Matt Westcot

Special thanks on the 2nd and 3rd editions to:

Ryan Berber, Josh Pinkerton, Zafar Jafri, Bradford Benner, Barbara Benner, Kurt Eggerling, Petr Duba, and Kisik Lee

Digital edition production:

Petr Duba, Rebecca Springer, Lindsay Seligman, and Teresa Sabatine

Astra Archery
2127 Olympic Parkway
Suite 1006 #158
Chula Vista, CA 91915

www.AstraArchery.com

ISBN 978-0-9824265-3-1 (3rd edition)
ISBN 978-0-9824265-2-4 (2nd edition)
ISBN 978-0-9824265-0-0 (1st edition)
ISBN 978-TK (ebook)

Contents

About the Authors

KiSik Lee

KiSik Lee is a man who hardly needs an introduction. His athletes have won dozens of medals at Olympic and World competitions and set countless world records. Lee has established himself while coaching in Korea, Australia, and the United States, making him a true citizen of the world. His decorated career and 40+ years of experience as a coach make him the premier global voice of archery technique.

Lee currently lives in Chula Vista, California, where he serves as the Head Coach for the United States of America at the Easton Archery Center of Excellence, located at the Chula Vista Elite Athlete Training Center.

Tyler Benner

Despite having a family steeped in archery history, his grandfather having been a champion field archer during the heyday '60s, Tyler did not start shooting until he was 14 years old. Forever the inquisitive mind, Tyler continually sought the correct words and explanations to describe the sport he loved. After attending Claremont McKenna College, dual majoring in Physics and Philosophy, and publishing a series of research projects on the harmonics of archery, Tyler moved to the US Olympic Training Center in Chula Vista, California, to train full-time with KiSik Lee. A kinship grew between the two of them, a powerful relationship seen best through the creation of the book, Total Archery – Inside the Archer, a collaboration between the master, Lee, and the student, Benner. Tyler is now pursuing writing, photography, and entrepreneurialism.

ABOUT THE AUTHORS

Foreword - Park Kyung-Mo

Olympic Gold Medalist

KiSik Lee, an innovative and respected coach of archery science, is a leader to many world-class archers and coaches. His archery philosophy is modern and cutting edge, yet hails from critical analysis of ancient techniques, including Korean traditional archery. Through Lee's coaching, seminars, and books, the world has come to a greater understanding of biomechanically correct archery technique. Elite archers shooting biomechanically efficient techniques are ensured consistency, strength, and longevity.

Lee's insistence on proper technique makes for beautiful archery. Beautiful archery is championship archery, and Lee understands better than anyone that there can be no compromise in beauty. Clearly then, an archer cannot compromise on technique, or on the practice necessary to develop technique.

Total Archery - Inside the Archer is a long awaited book from KiSik Lee, following his previous title, Total Archery. This book is a must-read for all current and prospective archers and coaches. Throughout this book, readers are in for an amazing experience that spreads a level of coaching never before seen. I believe Inside the Archer will be a catalyst for a new generation of archers shooting scores never before dreamed possible.

There is always room for improvement – even if you are a top ranking archer or coach. Those who have perseverance and determination to learn from this book will grow to be a master of our beloved sport! Along with Total Archery, Inside the Archer has every trait to be a valuable resource for generations of archers and coaches, long into the future. All the best in your journey!

His student,

박 경 모

PARK Kyung-Mo

FOREWORD - PARK KYUNG-MO

Foreword – Park Sung-Hyun

Olympic Gold Medalist and FITA World Record Holder – 1,405

The archery world is very excited to hear about KiSik Lee's newest publication, Total Archery – Inside the Archer. His first book, Total Archery, now translated into seven different languages, continues to be a remarkable benefit to archers and coaches around the globe. There have been many shooting manuals written in the past, however they always leave the reader with as many questions as answers. Inside the Archer attempts to address all those unanswered questions and will provide even the most technically inclined archers with the guidance they need to elevate their archery skill to the highest level. Inside the Archer will thrill even the most knowledgeable reader.

Lee's co-author and student, Tyler Benner, greatly enhances the archer's interpretation of technique. Because it is written from an archer's perception of feeling, this book is intended to be taken to the shooting range. It can be read from beginning to end, or as needed for specific answers. Inside the Archer will provide the path for any reader to learn a consistent method of shooting a recurve bow. No detail is left out!

KiSik Lee has studied human anatomy and biomechanics for decades, a study that has culminated in his wedding of the recurve bow to the natural workings of human anatomy. Inside the Archer will guide the reader through intricacies of efficiently using one's body to make a consistent and biomechanically correct shot. Mastering this technique will greatly reduce unwanted injuries.

Since neither the human body nor the recurve bow are likely to do much changing in the future, Inside the Archer may well be the final word on how to shoot the recurve bow.

I want to thank Coach Lee for his desire to share valuable knowledge with the world.

PARK Sung-Hyun

FOREWORD - PARK SUNG-HYUN

Introduction

Archery is an honest sport. Other sports have luck as the deciding factor between winners and losers. When luck is involved, reflecting on winning and losing is impossible because the pure moment is always cloudy. With archery, this is not the case. Whatever you do, you will see the answer on the target. It is this honesty, this transparency, which makes archery one of the last remaining pure sports. Yes, a judge can make a difference, but an archer's fate is always his own doing. In the end, that is what drew me to archery the most.

I first started shooting when I was fifteen or sixteen, at the beginning of high school. The funny thing is that I hated sports and I hated competing, and so the reason why I chose archery is I did not believe it was a sport. To me, it was more like a martial art. In time, I grew to enjoy competition, but I did not start archery as a sport. It was training for me, by myself, for my life.

My first exposure to archery was as a little boy, not yet ten years old. My father was very involved in shooting the Korean traditional bow, and I followed him several times to the range to watch his practice. I stayed beside him, listened to what he had to say, and just allowed archery to go on around me. I knew archery was more than a sport – it was an art, a martial art. That was a very big influence for me.

So when I first shot a bow and arrow, I was at high school. I had watched a practice a few days earlier and my teacher noticed that my eyes danced with the flying arrows. He asked me to try it, and straight away I wanted to do it because I knew it was what I liked. For me, archery does not have too much competition. In other sports, I see too much competitiveness. It makes some people barely human – not right – and certainly not whole. These people compete with each other too much, attacking those around them, and the only reason: winning. However, in archery, winning is different. Competition is different. This point is always there in my mind. One does not learn this just from doing archery. Even before I tried it, I knew it was an art from watching my father. When I became a coach, because I could help people, I saw how this art could truly change people's lives. This change happens not only because this sport is very difficult, especially to maintain performance every day, it happens because this sport predisposes one to being patient.

I would not say I am a patient man, but I am always learning from my archery career. I felt like I learned a lot when I was an archer, but I would say I have learned 100 times more from coaching. To me, coaching is a very patient job. When I shot, I only had to deal with myself, with my emotions, my control. But when you are coaching, you need to deal with every person, with everyone's level of patience, and with all of their differences. To me, archery is a great sport because you can learn that kind of patience, either as a coach or as an archer.

I would not have always described archery as being a sport of honesty. But after I became a coach and I saw my archers fighting their battles, then I could see it. I could see through their lies to themselves, and slowly, I could see how those old ideas melted away as they became more honest inside their hearts. This is one of my happiest memories because I could see how archery was changing them. Even though I was not telling them to change their hearts, they learned themselves – from archery! Now, whenever people learn this kind of lesson, they become a better person, a better shooter, and a better competitor. This is the greatest prize for me, to see people growing in this way.

Inside the Archer is a special book that is the continuation of my desire to spread archery throughout the world: to witness how archery changes lives. It builds on the principles originally set in Total Archery, and is the second in a trilogy of books that encompasses theory, technique, and coaching. No one book tells the whole story – Inside the Archer builds off of Total Archery, just like my future book on coaching will, too. I have been very happy to work with Tyler Benner on this book because I do not think anyone else in the world could have written as he has. He trained under me for over two years at the USA Olympic Training Center and not a day went by that he was not asking questions, writing notes, and studying video. He continually found new words and explanations that have refined my message and teachings. We will all become better archers because of Tyler's ability to find the true essence of technique and convey its spirit through words.

You still might be wondering what honesty in archery is. To this, I can only say that being honest means: you are honest – honest with your performance as the archer, the artist, and not with where your arrows hit on the target. I always tell my archers, "Throw one arrow! Throw it away! Just miss the target! One arrow, try to miss the target!" Because if that is what it takes, for my archer to aim away from his fear and shoot an arrow into the grass for the freedom of shooting one beautiful arrow, without caring where it goes, then that is what he must do. The arrow is not lying. The arrow never lies to you! Whatever you do, the arrow is the answer. But people will not accept that. They just say, "I am doing everything, I am shooting correctly, but the bow and the equipment is not right." These people blame everything but themselves, but that is not the way of archery!

This is why archery is a sport of honesty. Whatever you do, the arrow is the answer. If you shoot well, the arrows will group. If you do not shoot well, the arrows will not group. It is not equipment, not anything – just you. As long as you know this truth, you can be a great champion.

How to Read
this Book

———————

The following 26 chapters look deeply into individual segments of technique. There are two additional chapters that wrap up the important messages into summary points, however skipping to the end without reading the main course is like diving into dessert without eating dinner: sweet and pleasant for the first few bites, but ultimately lacking in the ability to actually be filling. As a whole, the book completes a full portrait of the archer. The individual chapters are arranged to walk the archer through the process of shooting. Pictures are used at great length to present additional material, or simply to provide visual representation of the topics discussed in the text. Reviews at the end of each chapter capture main ideas and help to blend the messages of multiple chapters together. For the sake of ease in phrasing, Inside the Archer predominantly addresses a gender-neutral male archer. It is only when the text specifically speaks about a picture of a female archer that feminine pronouns are used.

There is more information in this book than can be absorbed in a single read. To garner the most benefits from this text, it is advised to take a three-way approach. First, it is best to give either each chapter, or the whole book, a quick skimming read. This first read will expose most of the main ideas and provide shape and cohesion. Second, go back and examine the pictures in closer detail. Notice some of the subtleties in the lines and shapes drawn on the pictured archers. Lastly, give each chapter a thorough read. There is a lot of detail that should satisfy even the most discerning archers and coaches.

To all the archers reading this book, please realize this book was written for you. The title of the book, Inside the Archer, is meant to relate the feeling, emotion, and power one feels while shooting. Pay close attention to the words and phrases used to describe various techniques because even the slightest change in mental understanding can make all the difference. The difference is in the details.

Though this book is written from the feeling and understanding of an archer, coaches too, will find the text a valuable read. First and foremost, the descriptions are written either from an archer's perspective or toward an archer's feeling. However, it is the job of the coach to get inside of his archer. It is impossible for a coach to shoot the arrows for his students, but hopefully through these chapters coaches will feel more like their archers, and together the archer and coach can come closer together in their under-standing. If a coach remembers that in order for his archer to shoot a ten from 70 meters, the archer must keep the point of his arrow in a circle smaller than the tip of a ball-point pen, and then approach coaching with that same amount of precision and attention to detail, coaches can be assured much greater success. Too often the coach's acceptance of mediocrity is far greater than that of his archers. Sadly, most archers do not realize this travesty until it is too late. As a coach, you must level with yourself. Do you want your archers to shoot all their arrows in the gold? Do you coach them with equal precision and self-discipline? Are the words you choose to speak to them precisely the words needed to impart comprehension?

The goal of this book was to create a detailed portrait of archery that guides a pupil to transcend his technique and truly immerse himself in the brief moment of release. To become an Olympic Champion, this is what is required – total immersion of technique such that the motions become more than a means to an end, and become an end themselves. Archers must shoot beautifully to achieve beautiful results. Inside the Archer teaches beautiful technique with the hope that one day the reader will be able to shoot with more than just his technique. If every step is blindly followed, the archer will look like an automaton, a choppy archery robot that is only capable of following simple instructions. It is foolhardy to imagine every archer should look exactly the same. This book is filled with hundreds of photographs from almost two-dozen archers, all of them of different age, size, and sex. No two archers look exactly the same. This does not mean that technique does not matter, for this is just as foolhardy as saying everyone must shoot the same way. Inside the Archer carefully identifies core concepts that should be followed, resulting in archers of somewhat similar technical appearance. These concepts serve as the foundation of archery. Of course there is wiggle room, for every Olympic Champion has not followed exactly the same path. This is where an archer's flair can express itself. This is where archery gets interesting.

Hopefully the messages of this book fall on attentive ears, as a teacher cannot teach a pupil who is not listening. Be patient – you have many more lonely walks down to the target and back. At the moment of release, the imaginary becomes reality, and honesty is the only way of knowing why the arrow went in the middle of the target. Even a bulls-eye can sometimes be a mistake.

1   Stance

The feet serve as the foundation for the archer's power and posture. How one places his feet on the ground and the weight proportion positioning is known as the stance.

The modern method of stance, commonly known as "open stance," creates torsional stability through the hips and abdomen for greater consistency and strength down through the archer's feet, thereby establishing the correct foundation for the shot. The following description borrows no explanations from previously known depictions of the "open stance" and will stand alone as the "KSL open stance."

Placed equidistant on either side of the shooting line, the feet should be approximately shoulder-width apart. To take a slightly wider stance is acceptable, however no more than 4 centimeters wider than the width of the shoulders. Maintaining this distance keeps the archer centered over his body in a ready-athletic position.

FIGURE 1.1

This archer utilizes an open stance to create torsional stability through her midsection. Pay close attention to the direction of the feet, hips, and shoulders.

Correct placement and angle

Incorrect angle

FIGURE 1.2

This picture shows correct direction of the feet. While not completely parallel, they are almost so. A mistake is to open up the rear foot too much (if the toes pointed with the solid red arrow). Also notice how the feet are equidistant from the shooting line.

FIGURE 1.3

This photo shows incorrect feet positioning in the mentioned "duck feet" type open stance. Putting the feet in a v-shape creates excess strain on the knee joints and does not stabilize the weight shifts of the body as quickly.

To find the correct direction of the feet for the stance, start off by placing an arrow on the ground pointing straight at the target. Position the archer's toes on the edge of the arrow with his feet perpendicular to the shaft. Then, for right handed archers, rotate the front of the arrow approximately 30 degrees to the left, making an angle from the previous straight line. Exactitude is not important, however the resulting angle should not exceed 45 degrees. Left handed archers will move the arrow to the right of the target. This second line indicates the position of the forward foot and is what characterizes an open stance: the hips and feet are opened to the target. The archer places his toes on this new line, with his feet perpendicular to the repositioned arrow. Notice the toes are pointed in the same direction – one does not want duck feet – the feet should not take a v-shape. See figure 1.2 for correct positioning.

Three or four weeks later, or about 2000 arrows, after the archer has established comfort and consistency with the feet open to this angle, changes can be made for clearance or flexibility issues. A good rule of thumb is to have a straight line toward the target starting at the rear heel, (the right foot for a right handed archer), and running through the ball of the front foot. This is the most common and comfortable position for the feet. Gradually reduce the openness of the stance until the archer achieves maximum comfort. Most archers settle so that a straight line to the target could be drawn from rear the heel through the ball of the front foot.

FIGURE 1.4

Here we can see the pressure distribution across the feet. The brighter circles represent 60% of the weight properly balanced on the balls of the feet, while the lighter circles represent 40% of the weight on the heels. When thinking of the weight as distributed across these two focal points, it is important to remember that the entire foot is used in the balance. As 60% of the weight is forward on the balls of the feet, this means that even the toes will slightly grip the ground for stability and support.

Once the archer has established his foot placement, he must then distribute his weight correctly over the feet. For the KSL open stance, one should have approximately 60 percent of his weight on the balls of his feet, 40 percent on the heels. The proper proportion gives the archer the sensation of leaning slightly forward, thus having more pressure on the front of the feet rather than feeling as if there is less pressure on the heels. The forward pressure must not be so great as to bring the heels off the ground, however the archer should feel the edges of the toes carry some weight. Feeling all ten toes just slightly holding onto the ground is a good indication of the correctly balanced weight distribution, so long as the heels do not threaten to lift off the ground as a result.

The correct weight distribution cannot be achieved and maintained without the correct posture – pelvic tilt, flat back, and abdominal power control – so read this chapter very closely in conjunction with Chapter 2, "Posture," to ensure understanding. The goal of the stance is to connect the archer to the ground. The other elements of posture stem from the stance, and are thus also connected to the stillness of the ground when the archer maintains his internal connections and linkages. The archer can establish great stillness and strength simply by standing still, maintaining connection throughout his body, establishing the correct weight distribution on his feet, and feeling the energy of the ground flow into him.

The correct shoe is important to achieve the correct weight distribution. Many athletic shoes, especially running shoes, have an elevated heel that pitches the wearer forward. These are to be avoided, as they can curve the back and disconnect the archer from his abdominal strength. Too much weight on the balls of the feet can be just as bad as too little. A lightweight, flat, flexible, thin-soled shoe with a wide toe box to allow toe splay will make it much easier to achieve the correct weight distribution. When buying shoes for archery, one should mimic shooting motions while trying on many pairs. Boots generally have raised heels like running shoes and are discouraged for shooting. If weather is a factor, rubber shoe-covers offer the best protection-to-performance value proposition.

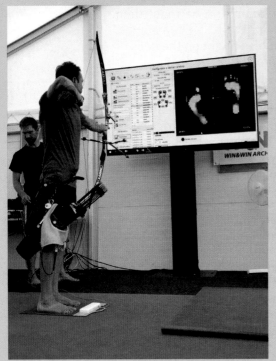

FIGURE 1.5

This image shows an archer standing on a pressure mat so you can see the importance of the big toe and using the entire foot to stabilize. Mats like this can also be used to evaluate foot health, fallen arches, or weak toes and intrinsic foot muscles. Good archers need strong feet. The proper pressure shape should extend from the heel, have a raised arch, and a pronounced big toe – just like if you learn to run in sandals.

Review

The stance serves as the foundation for all other technique elements. Without comfortable and correct foot positioning, it is impossible to draw power from the stillness of the ground. Stance is very closely tied to the subject of Chapter 2, "Posture," as these two elements of technique are the grounding, most fundamental elements of the archer's pose for shooting.

The key elements to remember about stance are:

• stance alignment 30 degrees open to the target

• the big toes should point roughly parallel

• 60/40 ratio of weight spread out across the entire foot in a natural foot shape with lifted arc

• find lightweight, flat, flexible, thin-soled shoes with a wide toe box to allow toe splay

• even the toes grip the ground (especially the big toe)

The stance is also closely tied to "Hip Alignment," Chapter 3, and "Shoulder Alignment," Chapter 21. The open stance forces the archer to twist through the torso to create the correct shoulder alignment, thus creating torsional stability through the trunk. The amount of openness to the stance affects head positioning (Chapter 6), as some archers struggle to achieve sufficient head rotation. Clearly, there is a maximum amount of comfortable rotation possible between the feet and hips in one direction, the shoulders twisted in another, and the head twisted back against the direction of the shoulders. Making small adjustments to the stance can affect the positioning of all the other alignments involved in the shooter's pose.

2 Posture

Deriving from the martial arts, correct archery posture focuses the intensity of the body deep into the core, from where great strength and control can then be directed outwards.

For the purposes of this chapter, posture will only be used to describe the positioning of the archer's back, core, hips and shoulders, and the overall orientation of the archer's body. Chapter 1, "Stance," concerning lower-body posture, and Chapter 21, "Shoulder Alignment," concerning upper-body posture, cover more aspects of how to stand and should be read concomitantly with this chapter.

The first key element of posture for high-performance archery is to tuck the hips down and forward. If the hips are properly tucked, the legs remain straight with no bend in the knees. Do not bend the knees, but also do not forcefully lock them out, as doing so can lead to unwanted tension in the body. To think about tucking the hips down, the archer should thrust the hips slightly forward and imagine holding a quarter between the cheeks of the buttocks. The stomach muscles, also, must be tensed, holding the power deep in the abdomen below the waist line. While shooting, this makes the stomach slightly protrude and eliminates nearly all curve to the lower back. See figure 2.1 for an example of tucked hips, tensed abdomen and buttocks, and the resultant straight spine.

FIGURE 2.1

Notice the slightly protruding stomach, despite the archer's lean frame, and that the bones of the chest are more in and down than are the stomach muscles. This archer has allowed the power of his core to fill his stomach until there is a tight feeling. This tightness gives him great strength to draw and control the bow. Also notice how a line (the yellow line) drawn straight down from where the string touches the archer's chin is the furthest lateral position. With incorrect posture, the line would touch the chest, stomach, or hips.

Hollow back, raised chest and untucked hips

Position of power: tucked hips, slightly protruding stomach, and tucked rib cage

FIGURE 2.2

Notice the extreme difference in posture between these two pictures. In the left picture, the weight is on the heels, the hips are out, and the chest is raised. In the picture on the right we can clearly see the powerful connections of the archer through her torso. Notice the straight spine in the right picture.

The second key element of posture is to use the abdomen to hold the ribcage down. While easy to do at the set position, as described at greater length in Chapter 8, keeping the ribcage down becomes much more difficult as the archer begins to raise his arms to draw the bow. An archer commonly becomes disconnected with his stomach and allows the ribcage to rise with the upward motion of raising the bow. As soon as this disconnection happens it is impossible to shoot a strong, balanced shot, because all the focusing, controlling power of the body comes from within the core. Perfect practice makes perfect, and archers are advised to begin practicing in front of the mirror, watching their chest and abdomen for any movement while raising the bow at the target.

FIGURE 2.3

Notice how the archer's weight is too much on his heels, and that there is more weight on his left foot than his right. This example of poor posture goes from the lower body up. The archer is leaning back and his power is disconnected.

FIGURE 2.4

This picture shows the same archer with corrected posture. The weight is more forward on the balls of the feet, the head position is more forward and out over the chest, and the weight is even on both feet. Notice the archer does not have the duck feet he had in figure 2.3. The bulge in his back is actually his scapula winging away from his body, not a result of a curved spine. This is correct positioning.

It is especially important for the archer to feel the power and intensity of his body just below the waistline, deep inside the stomach. The connection of the muscles in the back to the muscles deep in the stomach is the very same intensity and power used to expand through the clicker. To maintain the strength and direction necessary to keep shoulder alignment through the shot and follow-through, the same core strength must be used. Only through correct focus and posture can the archer achieve these connections. See Chapter 10, "Angular Motion," and Chapter 18, "Release," for more discussions on shoulder alignment during execution.

As was covered in Chapter 1, "Stance," 60 percent of the weight of the body should be moved onto the balls of the feet, with 40 percent remaining on the heels. The archer should not be leaning forward (bending at the waist or out on the toes), but the power and force of his body must be forward (feeling the toes grip the ground while the heels remain in contact). Archers often incorrectly begin leaning backwards while loading, anchor, transferring, or expanding. To lean back is to disconnect from the power of the body, and will cause inconsistent, weak shots, and left and right arrows.

FIGURE 2.5

This picture helps to show some of the muscles talked about for shooting. The white shape represents the scapula, which is a bone. The green shape represents the upper-trapezius, the blue is the rhomboid, pink is teres major, and the red is the lower-trapezius. The yellow shape represents the abdominal strength through the stomach muscles and the intercostals. Underneath the muscles shown in the thoracic spine region, directly beside the spine, are the paraspinals.

A tiny lean would be a difference of shifting the weight balance back from a 60/40 ratio to a 55/45 ratio. As the pressure on the feet changes, so, too, the posture changes, and therefore the entire force of the body. Posture must be maintained during the entire drawing and shooting of the bow.

Because the core strength and holding of the abdominal muscles is stressed so much in conventional coaching, many archers will overcompensate. Overcompensating archers typically look as if they are performing a tiny crunch, leaning slightly forward at the waist. The body is out of alignment and the archer has created a weak position. The correct tightening of the abdominal muscles is not as much a crunch as it is a shifting of power down. Think of it as someone placing two hands on either side of the ribs and pushing straight down toward the feet. The archer must not lean forward; the archer must not lean back. The core must remain over the feet, as correct posture depends on maintaining the 60/40 weight-distribution ratio.

The most common cause of incorrect posture is an arched or 'hollow' back. When the shoulders rise up as the archer points toward the target, the abdominal muscles begin to relax. Generally, the buttocks begin to stick out as a result. See figures 2.2 and 2.3 for examples of hollow backs. A common ailment of archers who shoot with an arched or hollow back is a high full-draw elbow position. Recall that when the chest is lifted up the shoulders come up too, disconnecting the archer from the strong muscles around the thoracic spine, and specifically from the lower trapezius muscle. When the chest is properly kept lowered, the edge of the scapula is also pulled down by muscle activation lower in the back. As the scapula is connected to the shoulder, and the shoulder to the drawing elbow, lowering the scapula position also lowers the elbow at full-draw until it approaches the optimal alignment: parallel with the arrow.

Another critical element of posture is borrowed from weightlifting. Especially when doing a squat, weightlifters will fill their abdomen and chest with air and expand outwards until there is a great sensation of tightness. Prior to lifting the bow, an archer should expand his diaphragm outwards, filling the lungs part-way with air, holding a sensation of tightness throughout his core. This can be thought of as allowing his power to fill him. The tightness could also be described as a 'full' sensation, as though the archer could not comfortably expand his stomach or chest much further. Look back to figure 2.1 to see the fullness of the archer's stomach. Despite the fullness, one can see all the muscles of the abdomen are still tight.

Subtle changes in posture can create big differences in shooting, comfort, and control. Seeing inconsistencies in weight distribution, the overall sense of calm, tension, or lack thereof, and power within the archer takes a very trained and perceptive eye. Posture must be closely monitored and compared back to previous months to notice significant progression.

FIGURE 2.6

Even through the moment of release the posture must be held deep in the body's core, keeping the weight balanced over the feet and the spine held straight.

Review

A powerful posture must be used to create strength throughout the body. Although the posture pertains to the entire body, the most important areas that should be focused on are the hips, core, and chest/shoulders. With 24 movable vertebrae, there is considerable room for unintended shifts in posture. Power must be held deep in the abdomen to keep the spine flat, creating a strong center that energizes and stabilizes the rest of the body.

The key elements to remember about posture are:

• hips must be tucked forward to create a flat back

• the stomach muscles need to be tightened to hold the ribs and chest down

• the legs must be straight, but not locked

• the body's force should be forward, over the feet, with the 60/40 ratio from stance

• high elbow position often relates directly to a curved spine (hollow back)

• the head sits out over the chest, and is the farthest extended part of the body

It is easy to lose the connection of power with the abdomen while raising the bow at the target, as described in Chapter 8, "Set Position." When this disconnection happens, the spine will curve backwards, the chest will raise, and the ribs will stick out. It is also easy to lose the 60/40 balance ratio on the feet during drawing, as described in Chapter 11, "Drawing," Chapter 15, "Transfer," and Chapter 17, "Expansion."

Head positioning is very important to posture, as the head must be the furthest outward point if viewed from directly in front or behind the archer. The head must be positioned forward, out over the body. If a line extended down vertically from the contact point of the string to the chin touches any part of the body, a change in posture is needed.

Permanent changes in posture take time to implement, are often fairly subtle, and are best noticed when compared week to week, or even month to month. Day to day inconsistencies are sometimes difficult to notice, and controlling them demands patience and persistence from the archer. The ultimate goal is always to create a comfortable, powerful, and unchanging posture.

3   Hip Alignment

Hip alignment sets the direction of the lower half of the body and resists the twisting forces generated by correct shoulder alignment.

By keeping the hips open to the target but twisting the shoulders past the target (see also Chapter 21, "Shoulder Alignment"), archers are able to contain the powerful twisting force through the trunk of the body. Much as twisting a towel makes it stronger, or twisting pieces of grass together makes a rope, the twisting forces generated between the hips and shoulders allows the archer to hold his power deep in the abdomen with a strength he would not have if the torso were not twisted.

The same alignment that was established by the feet during the stance should be generally copied for the alignment of the hips. Where the feet are approximately a 30 degree angle open to the target, the hips will be 20-25 degrees open to the target. Some archers may be able to hold their hips at the same angle to the target as their feet, but doing so is not necessary. The key remains steadiness and consistency: once the archer has settled on a direction for his hips, that direction must be held for the duration of the shot. The actual angle of the hips may vary from archer to archer, but it must not vary in the same archer from shot to shot or day to day.

Very commonly an archer will slowly uncoil his hips as he draws the bow and holds and shoots. An archer who uncoils his hips is losing the connection from his body to the strength and power of the shot by giving away the powerful twist in the core. Strength is seeping out if the hips are de-rotating while drawing or holding the bow.

Positioning the hips requires a pelvic tilt down and forward. In a neutral standing position the pelvis is naturally up and out, the buttocks slightly protrude, and a natural curvature in the lower spine is noticeable. To position the hips for optimum shooting stabilization, one must tighten the buttocks as though attempting to hold a piece of paper or a coin between the muscles of the gluteus. Tuck the hips forward as if with a slight thrust. These two very small external motions are one, and serve to flatten the lower spine. If viewed with x-ray vision, the spine should appear almost completely flat all the way from the coccyx, or tailbone, to the bottom of the scapula.

In addition to flattening the spine, tucking the hips down and forward tightens the muscles of the abdomen, focusing the holding strength of the body deep within the core, just below the waist line. The position of the core is extremely critical to shooting, as it is the main source of power, calm, and control. An archer should look to this center of power when he needs to stabilize not only his body, but his mind as well.

The weight balance generated by tucking the hips forward should position the archer in the correct 60/40 ratio as described in Chapter 1, "Stance." It is possible to tuck the hips down and forward but still keep too much weight on the heels of the feet. The archer must periodically check his balance to make sure the correct ratio remains at the pedestal for his hip alignment: his feet.

FIGURE 3.1

Here we can see the direction of the hips, feet, and shoulders. The torso twists through the abdomen and chest, creating power from the torque. If the hips lose their direction and begin turning towards the target, body control will be lost along with the 60/40 weight-proportion balance described in Chapter 1. The yellow line represents where the archer is twisting through his core to achieve correct shoulder alignment.

3 HIP ALIGNMENT

FIGURE 3.2

Direction at the target is indicated by the arrow on the bowstring. Contrast this angle with the lines indicating the hips and feet. To maintain this much twist the archer must hold a great deal of strength deep in his stomach and core.

Review

Hip alignment is critical to creating a torsionally stabilized core. With a direction similar to the alignment of the feet, the hips control the lower half of the body, and hold the power of the ground to resist the twisting forces of the shoulders. By tucking the hips down and forward, extra strength is added to the core allowing the archer to access power deep in his body.

The key elements to remember about hip alignment are:

• hips must be tucked down and forward to create a flat back

• the hip and feet alignment should be approximately similar, 30 degrees for the feet and 20-25 degrees for the hips

• 60/40 balance ratio must be maintained with the correct pelvic tilt

• hip alignment should not change during the shot as it directly results in a loss of power in the abdomen, subsequently creating a weak feeling throughout the body

Hip alignment is related to the feet alignment, Chapter 1, and works in conjunction with "Shoulder alignment," Chapter 21, to create a powerful twist in the trunk of the body. This twist helps the archer to maintain stability while shooting, especially in windy conditions. The common problem is for the archer to lose hip alignment relative to shoulder alignment, as it takes considerable strength, control, and focus to maintain these opposed positions.

4   Hooking

The act of curling one's fingers around the string is the first permanent reference point attaching the archer to the bow.

There are only two places the archer comes in contact with the bow: through the string with hooking, and through the grip at the bow hand. Because these two positions, hooking and grip positioning, are the only ways the archer interacts with the bow, these elements are critical – any inconsistencies or mistakes in other technique elements will be compounded here. The entire pressure of the bow meets the archer where he hooks the string and where he grips with the bow hand. Incorrect finger placement on the string can result in painful blisters, corns, or abrasions that end careers in archery before they even start. Great care is needed for the details of hooking not only to ensure the greatest possible accuracy, but also to ensure longevity in the sport.

The most overlooked mainstay of hooking is the importance of hooking upwards, especially with the top or index finger. If viewed directly from the side, the fingernail of the top finger should point slightly upwards, toward the sky. Most archers do the opposite and hook downwards, effectively losing all top finger pressure and control. See figure 4.1 for examples of hooking upwards and hooking downwards.

Only when hooked upwards can the top finger have the correct pressure and direction to give the archer the sharpest, most cutting release. Mastering the upward hook until a locking sensation is achieved will free the archer from many common problems like inconsistent pressure or the string sliding through the fingers. To think of hooking upwards another way, remember that the bottom side of the top finger, the edge closest

Correct – Hooking upward   **Incorrect – Hooking downward**

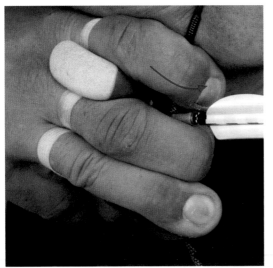 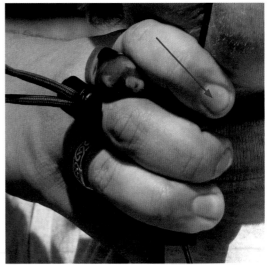

FIGURE 4.1

The key finger is the top finger. One must squeeze the finger spacer between the index and middle fingers to allow the top finger to hook upwards, toward the jaw.

Notice on the incorrect example how the top finger points down at the throat. On the correct example, see how the finger hooks along the jaw, toward the chin.

to the middle finger, is where all of the pressure should be felt. Squeeze the finger spacer at the base of the fingers, so that the top finger has the angle beyond the knuckle to hook upwards toward the chin. Refer again to figure 4.1, and to figure 4.3, to see how the upper half of the top finger does not touch the string when the archer is hooking correctly. Hooking upward ensures clearance between the top and middle fingers, making it impossible for the archer to pinch the arrow. If the archer is having trouble pinching the arrow, or finds his top finger continues to make contact with the arrow, the problem surely will be solved when he masters correctly hooking upwards. See figure 4.2 for acceptable clearance of the top finger over the arrow.

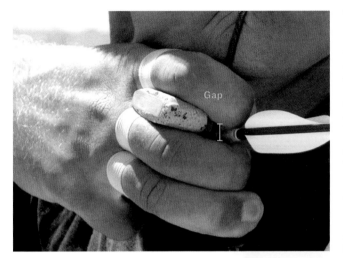

FIGURE 4.2

This photo shows correct hooking of the top finger and an acceptable gap between the top finger and the arrow. Notice that it isn't much, barely more than a millimeter. A wider gap is difficult to achieve, and is unnecessary. With a smaller gap, the top finger will rest against the arrow. When first hooking the string, the middle finger may touch the arrow. Upon drawing the bow, the arrow will naturally rise toward the top finger as the string bends. Proper positioning can be seen in many pictures throughout this book. Also notice the positioning of the bottom finger. It still is securely on the string, however it does not hook like the top two fingers. The third finger cannot be allowed to slip off the string as it stabilizes the twist of the hand.

FIGURE 4.3

Here we see the string positioning on the fingers. The string is in front of the joint on the top finger, in the joint on the middle finger, and in front of the joint on the third finger. The thumb stretches down and back. The top two finger positions should be the same on nearly all archers. Only the third finger position will be different. Also, the yellow shape on the top and middle fingers shows that the pressure on the top two fingers should be felt exclusively in the bottom half of the fingers. We can see a slight upward turn of the top and middle fingers.

The second most important element of hooking is the string position as relative to all the joints of the fingers. Again, the top finger is the most important to position correctly, as it sets the standard for the rest of the fingers. The string should be placed 2-4 millimeters in front of the last joint on the top finger, toward the end of the finger. See figure 4.3 for an illustration of the string's position on the fingers. Once hooking is complete the string should not move, slide, or change from this position. Hooking in the joint of the top finger may make the joint very sore and stiff or develop a corn under the skin. For reasons that are not entirely understood, the middle finger may be hooked in the joint and will not suffer from these problems. It becomes considerably more difficult to achieve clean and fast releases should the archer attempt hooking deeper than is suggested here. The position of the string on the top finger should be exactly the same for all archers, while the positions of the middle and third fingers vary depending on the length of the individual archer's fingers. With the string in the correct position on the top finger, it will fall either in the joint of the middle finger or just behind the joint.

FIGURE 4.4

It is very important to visually check the hooking position rather than just attempt to feel it with the fingers. Also notice the comfortable position the archer is in here: bent bow arm and relaxed demeanor.

FIGURE 4.5

As the bow is drawn, the angle of the string changes in the archer's hand. Because of the angle change, the pressure felt on the individual fingers will change. At the setup position, the left photo, the archer should feel 80 percent of the pressure on his top finger. All the way back at full draw, the photo on the right, he should only feel approximately 40 percent on his top finger.

The string will sit in the middle of the pad on the third finger (see figure 4.3). If the archer hooks behind the joint with the middle finger (more common for male archers than female, owing to their larger variance of length between the top and middle fingers), they may begin to build up a small callus. It is advised to keep the hands moisturized so any calluses do not crack and split. Also, it is helpful to take a small nail file and abrade the calluses down to flush with the surrounding skin every week or two so they do not become unmanageable.

Numbness, tingling, and shooting pains up the arm are all caused by incorrect finger placement or pressure on the string. (A tab that is too thin may also cause these problems. A tab that feels too thick at first will often squash down to a comfortable thickness where as one that feels perfect right away will become too thin after a few thousand arrows.) Moving the string position by only a millimeter on one finger can be the difference between shooting in pain or comfort. As the positioning is so exacting and critical, archers should carefully inspect their string hooking each time they grab the string to ensure consistent finger positioning.

Correct – Thumb stretched back and wrist cocked out

Incorrect – Thumb forward and straight wrist

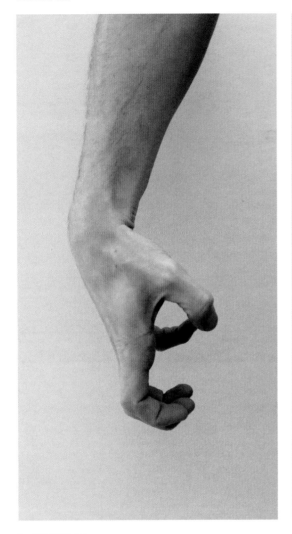
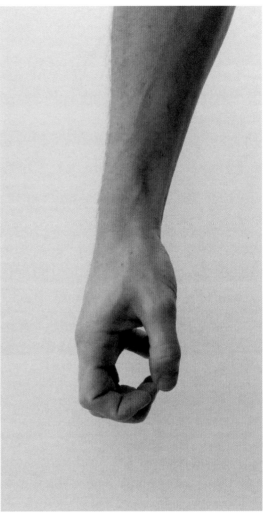

FIGURE 4.6

The natural wrist position is depicted in the picture on the left. This is where the forearm muscles are the most relaxed. In order to hold the positioning for the picture on the right, the thumb must be pushed forward with tension held in the arm.

Empirical evidence has found the most consistent positioning is achieved when the archer first touches the fingertips to the string, and then rolls the string into the correct position while hooking the fingers. The key element here is that the archer only makes one fluid movement with the fingers and never re-grips or double-takes on position. Some archers have an unconscious anxiety that causes mental anxiety until they re-grip the string, and will continue nervously re-gripping the string even while starting to draw the bow. These nervous ticks make it impossible to get consistent hooking.

Once the archer has set the position of the fingers on the string and transitions to placing his hand into the grip of the bow, he will eventually move all the way into "Set Position" detailed in Chapter 8. Now the archer can concern himself with the correct finger pressure. Remember that finger pressure is vastly different at full draw than it is at the set position: as the bow is drawn, the string takes a more and more acute angle. Where the string was nearly straight at set position, it now is bent 20 degrees in. This change of angle will change finger pressure, even though the archer does not change his amount of finger hooking (see figure 4.5 for clarification on the string bending around the fingers, changing the resultant pressures). So: at the set position, the archer should feel as if his top finger is holding 70 to 80 percent of the force of the bow.

Repeated again, the top finger is the most important finger. As the bow is drawn, more force will naturally be transfered to the other fingers even though the amount of hooking and the string position on the fingers do not change. At full draw the percentages should be roughly 50 percent middle finger, 40 percent top finger, and 10 percent bottom finger. If the set position finger pressure is established correctly, the full draw finger pressure will naturally approximate the correct ratio.

FIGURE 4.7

This picture focuses on the stretching of the fingers forward while stretching the thumb back at the same time. This makes a bend in the hand as shown by the red line. It also flattens the knuckles in a motion opposite of making a fist.

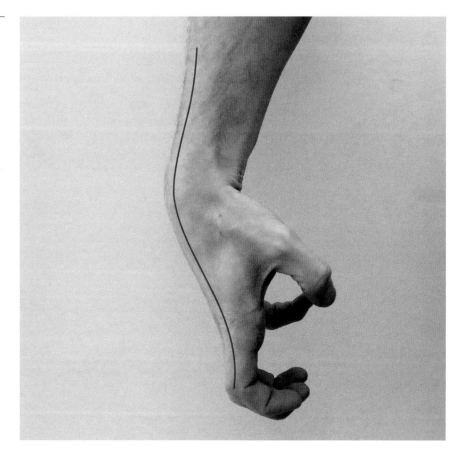

The amount of hooking, or the amount of finger curl – not to be confused with finger placement, how deep into the finger the string is placed – is relative to each finger. If viewed from directly in front of the archer, the fingernails should almost be invisible – the fingernails of the top two fingers should point back at the archer's throat, and not out to the side. The bottom finger does not hook as much as the others, and is instead used to stabilize the hand on the string and resist unwanted twisting. See figure 4.9. Once finger curl is established, it should not decrease in the slightest. Losing hooking at any moment while shooting is the primary way archers lose the connection with their backs and use push-pull techniques. Coaches often tell their archers to "keep a deep hook," but the distinction must be made that the archer is being told to curl his fingers slightly more, not change the position of the string to deeper in the finger.

To ensure the correct usage of the muscles of the back for drawing the bow, the thumb must be positioned such that it puts the muscles of the forearm in a relaxed position. In order to keep the forearm relaxed, the drawing hand thumb needs to be stretched down and back such that the web of skin between the thumb and forefinger is stretched mildly taut. The pinky should be stretched back and curl into the hand much like the thumb. Proper positioning of the pinky and thumb of the drawing hand comes up again in Chapter 13, "Anchor Position."

FIGURE 4.8

See in this picture how much the archer curls his top and middle fingers back towards his throat. Look at the fingernails, and note how it is only possible to see side profiles of them square to the chin. Contrast their positioning with the third finger which clearly displays the whole fingernail facing forward. Only by hooking this amount is it possible to have a very strong and tight anchor position, as is also shown by this picture and discussed fully in Chapter 13.

With the thumb stretched down and back, as in figure 4.7, the drawing wrist will appear bent outwards. Many archery texts in the past have incorrectly mandated a flat or straight drawing wrist, but, in fact, a bent wrist is the desired position. As an exercise, find a bucket, a grocery bag, or something the fingers can use to mimic holding a string. Hook the bucket with three fingers as though practicing a shooting position and relax the forearm and wrist as much as possible. The wrist will naturally bend out to the side as the hand/arm finds the equilibrium point, or the position of lowest energy. This exact same position of the wrist and hands, as seen in figure 4.6 and 4.7, should be used while shooting. With the forearm muscles at their lowest energy position, the powerful and stable muscles of the back and core will be able to hold the complete force of the bow without any unwanted interference from the hand, wrist, forearm, or shoulder. Drawing and shooting with a bent outwards wrist is also vitally important to preventing drawing shoulder impingement and injury. Archers that shoot with a straight or inwards bending wrist run the added risk of injury because the extra forearm muscle activation makes it more difficult to relax the biceps muscle, limiting their capacity for angular motion. A tight biceps muscle can easily cause impingement in the shoulder joint and damage the delicate spinatus or deltoid muscles where they attach to the humerus.

A final clarification on hand positioning that pertains to the outward appearance of the knuckles of the forefinger, middle, and ring fingers: many archers have a common problem that makes their middle knuckle protrude more than the index and ring finger knuckles. The problem is created by having incorrect string positioning and/or finger pressure. Generally, the more upwards the archer can hook with his index finger, the lesser degree of knuckle protrusion he will have. In fact, the knuckles should all be cocked inward so as to flex the tendons through the middle of the hand, making them visible. With the thumb flexed backward and the wrist sticking outwards, the center of the hand is opened up, keeping the power in the fingertips holding the string, ensuring the sharpest and most cutting release. Examine figures 4.7 and 4.8 for pictures clarifying the slightly flexed positioning of the drawing fingers.

All of this work in securing the correct positioning, hooking, and pressure of the fingers is for naught if these complex positions are not exactly maintained and held through the remaining processes of shooting. Though these pointers will ensure the most advantageous position for shooting, many archers around the world have used other approaches with great success. Some may argue it does not matter how one hooks the string, but they must agree with the over-arching concept: that the chosen position and pressure does not change. Archery is a sport of repetition – if one technique is replicated time and time again without any changes, then it is a successful implementation of technique. The traits of correct hooking described above will provide archers with techniques that are easiest to duplicate, especially under pressure, and are the most biomechanically correct positions for ensuring power, comfort, and longevity.

Review

As one of two places where the archer comes in contact with the bow, hooking is especially critical. All aspects of technique must funnel through this single element. Correct hooking will allow for good expansion (Chapter 17), sharp releases (Chapter 18), and will help the archer to maintain overall control while shooting. There is not a more helpless and out-of-control feeling in archery than if the archer senses his fingers slipping on the string and does not feel secure with his hook. Hooking sets the position of the drawing wrist and predetermines the hand position at anchor position. From a health standpoint, correct hooking is also very important as it is very easy to build up painful sores, blisters, or calluses that could permanently damage an archer's fingers.

FIGURE 4.9

This picture is very good for illustrating how much the hand is rotated compared to the arm and the wrist. Most archers will attempt to rotate their wrist to get better hooking on the string, however the rotation must occur in the hand and fingers and not in the wrist. See how the wrist and the elbow joint here have essentially the same angle. (There is nothing wrong with the archer's eyes – he is using a special set of contact lenses that function as sunglasses.)

The key elements to remember about hooking are:

• the top finger controls most of the principles of hooking

• hooking upwards is critical to correct wrist, hand and anchor positioning

• the string must sit just in front of the first joint of the top finger

• the fingertips should hook so much that the fingernails point backwards and upwards at the throat

• the top and middle fingers should squeeze the finger spacer – although counter-intuitive, this helps to create a larger space between the fingers for the arrow

• when first hooking the string prior to raising the bow, 80 percent of the force should be held with the top finger. As the string bends while being drawn, this ratio will change to approximately 40 percent on the top finger, 50 percent on the middle finger, and 10 percent on the bottom finger

• the thumb and pinky must be pulled back, stretching taut the skin between the thumb and forefinger

The wrist must relax and bend outwards in the natural position. Once established, hooking must remain constant and consistent. Changes in finger pressure, wrist bend, or hooking direction will change the force and direction of the release, as discussed in Chapter 18. A common problem is to lose the amount of hooking while drawing or coming to the loading position, causing inconsistent draw length and expansion. Finger strength should be built up during holding drills (Chapter 16), to ensure an unchanging positioning.

The 1000 Arrow Challenge

The 1000 arrow challenge is a test of both the mind and the body's ability to cope with pain, boredom, strength, and endurance. In one solid training session, archers will shoot 1000 arrows consecutively, a feat lasting easily eight hours. The fastest time on record is a few minutes more than six hours. At this rate, the record-setting archer knocked one arrow, shot it, and pulled it from the target every 21 seconds, for 1000 shots in a row. The ultimate test of the human body, technique, and biomechanics, only archers who shoot with correct form can maintain such a physical performance for eight hours straight. All of the techniques described in this book have stood up to the 1000 arrow challenge and have kept archers who use them effectively safe from injury. (Any archer attempting this should have professional supervision and months of prerequisite training to avoid injury).

Dozens of archers have all completed the 1000 arrow challenge without adverse physical effects. If 1000 arrows seems excessive for a single day, it is not for strength that archers attempt this grueling training experience. The psychological benefits are the biggest gains made during this difficult day. Shooting a 144-arrow FITA will have never before felt so easy. A 300 or 400 arrow training day will barely touch the physical and psychological depths an archer must reach to finish the 1000 arrow day. Even the most proud will find himself humbled by the ache in his fingers and the ever present thought, "Am I done yet?"

The 1000 arrow challenge is a wonderful capstone to mark the end of a long training cycle. By giving athletes a goal to strive towards, its successful completion can give anyone the confidence and maturity to step away for a few weeks. With a big task under the belt and some relaxation with loved ones, athletes can come back ready for competition.

It is hard enough to pull the bow back 1000 times, but pulling 1000 arrows out of the target is also quite a feat. When attempting the challenge, have a good target buttress and plenty of arrow lube nearby!

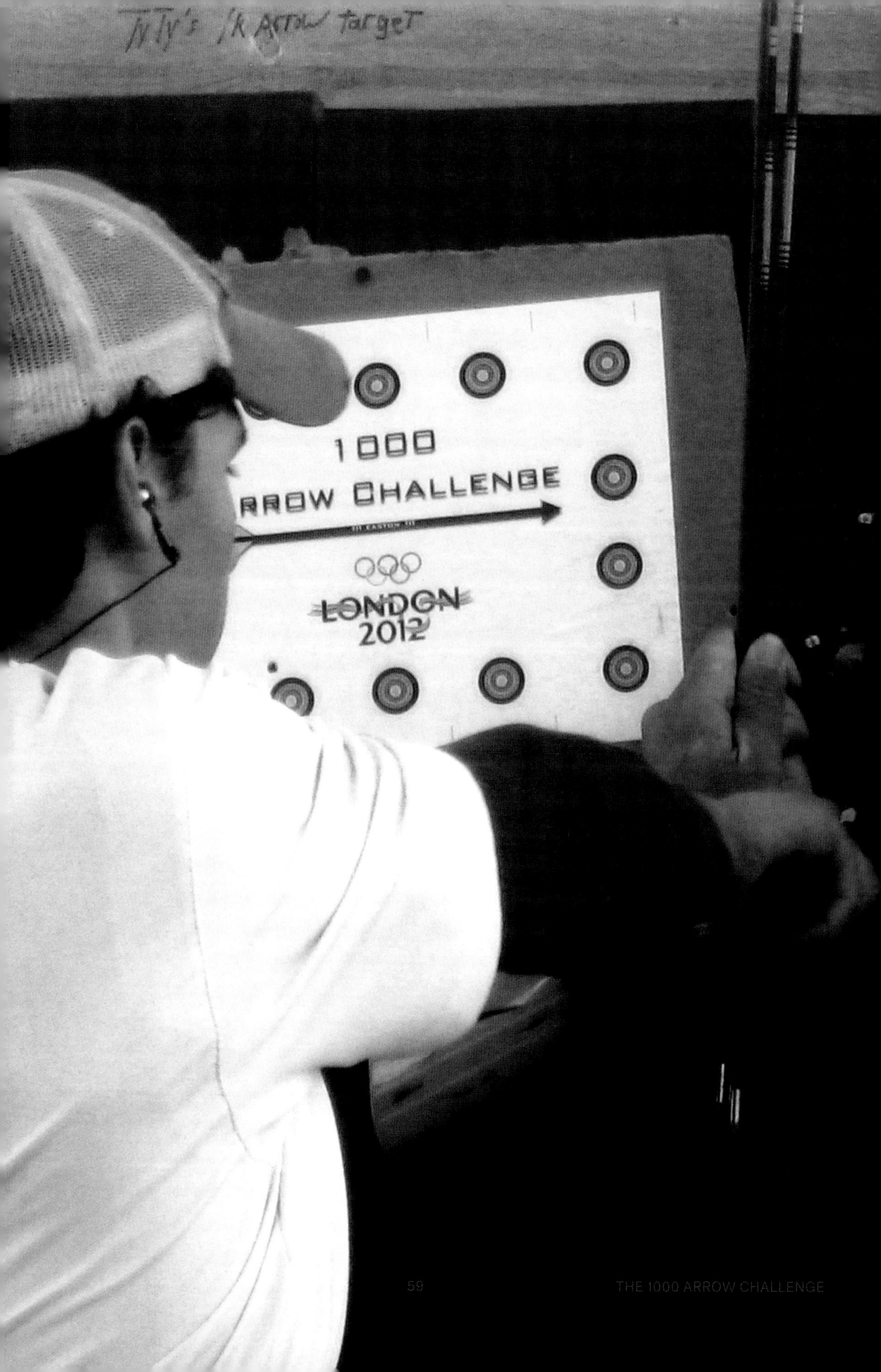
1000
RROW CHALLENGE
LONDON
2012

5   Grip Positioning

Placing one's hand in the grip of the bow creates the foundation of the forward balance of the shot.

Many archers neglect the importance of the holding balance, yet remember that half of the shot happens in the front half! Incorrect hand placement or pressure in the grip can fold an entire shot in half, no matter how perfect loading, anchor, transfer, or execution is completed. The balance of the front half of the shot all starts with the bow hand and correct placement and pressure in the grip.

Grip placement starts with the angle of the hand. First and foremost, the knuckles of the bow hand should be at least at a 45 degree angle to the vertical. Flexibility will be the determining factor for how flat an archer can position his knuckles. Archers with the ability to rotate their bow arm elbows more than normal will commonly also be able to achieve a flatter knuckle positioning on the grip. The elevation of the grip, too, whether or not the archer shoots a 'high' or a 'low' grip, depends on how much rotation is possible. Higher angles of knuckle positioning are possible with grip elevations that exceed 50 degrees from the vertical. This type of positioning places the hand and wrist into the most powerful and stable position, as well as helping provide maximum clearance for the string while allowing the arrow to oscillate freely as it comes out of the bow. See figure 5.1 for a few pictures of bow hands with acceptable angles.

70 degree angle to the bow – Good

Common 45-50 degree angle – OK

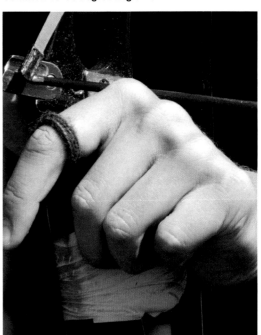

FIGURE 5.1

Both of these photos show acceptable degrees of knuckle angle to the riser. Archers learning this positioning must have at least the angle of the picture on the right. Flexibility is the limiting factor here because higher elevations than 45 degrees takes a good deal of strength, control, and joint mobility to establish. Grip positioning as indicated in figure 5.2 must not be compromised to achieve higher angles relative to the bow. One should not worry too much so long as a 45 degree angle is possible.

Hand placement and pressure point on the grip

Contact map and pressure point location on the hand

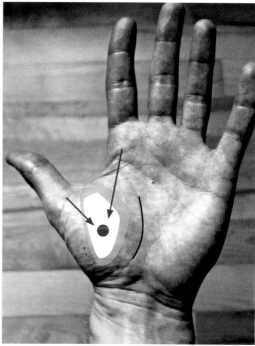

FIGURE 5.2

These pictures show the shape of grips for a right-handed archer. The grips have a slight bulge on the side to follow the lifeline of the hand. This creates a more stable launching platform for the bow. In both cases, the pressure point is highlighted in red. The black line shows the lifeline of the hand. The white shape represents the

secondary pressure point through the hand. The two red arrows show the direction of the hand bones of the thumb and forefinger, showing why the pressure point is located where it is. For a left handed archer, the pressure point and positioning on the grip apply in reverse.

To create the optimized hand angle, the edge of the grip needs to sit just at the edge of the lifeline in the bow hand. No part of the grip should sit past the lifeline of the hand. The throat of the grip fits between the thumb and index fingers in the fleshy part of the hand. With the throat of the grip bisecting the thumb and forefinger and the corner of the grip sitting just at the edge of the lifeline, this should create the desired 45 degree angle.

Hand placement is the basis of establishing a consistent and accurate grip. However correct hand pressure is what creates the true balance for the front half of the shot. The pressure point, or the main focal point of pressure, both on the hand and the grip, is where archers must concentrate their force. On the bow hand, the pressure point is located near the base of the thumb, midway between the lifeline and the outer edge of the hand. On the grip, the pressure point is located on the outer half of the grip, toward the plunger, midway down from the throat of the grip. See figure 5.2 for photos outlining the shape and location of the pressure point and the positioning in the hand.

5 GRIP POSITIONING

Pinky knuckle pulled very far back - Good   **More common amount of knuckle back - OK**

FIGURE 5.3

Both photos are correct positioning for the bow hand, however the photo on the left is a more extreme degree of pulling the pinky knuckle back toward the body. If it is possible to comfortably do this, this is a strong position.

It is acceptable if the archer is only able to duplicate the photo on the right. Some archers possess flexible wrists and are able to easily pull the knuckle very far back. So long as the pinky knuckle is entirely behind the line of the first.

With the pressure more directed to the outside half of the grip, the resulting pressure and angles will cause the bow string to jump more straight or slightly biased away from the bow arm, preventing injury from string slap, flinching, and collapsing. Nearly every weak shot is caused by a disconnection in the front half of the shot. With the correct pressure point and hand position in the grip, the archer will not be compelled to yank their release hand back faster or squeeze their back muscles with excessive intensity – common causes of weak shots.

Borrowing a word from Judo, the phenomenon in the correct hand placement and grip pressure can be called kumi. A judo fighter uses the power and direction in the core of their body and directs it through his grip, his kumi, to create an unbreakable connection to his opponent. The fighter with the stronger kumi controls the fight. Kumi is created by locking the elbow down, using the power at the base of the thumb to direct the power of the shoulder and body into the other, and bracing the arm and body as though it were a truss on a bridge. By using the one word kumi, a coach can remind his archer to refocus on the pressure point, make sure the hand-angle stays consistent, and to direct the energy for the shot from the body to provide balance.

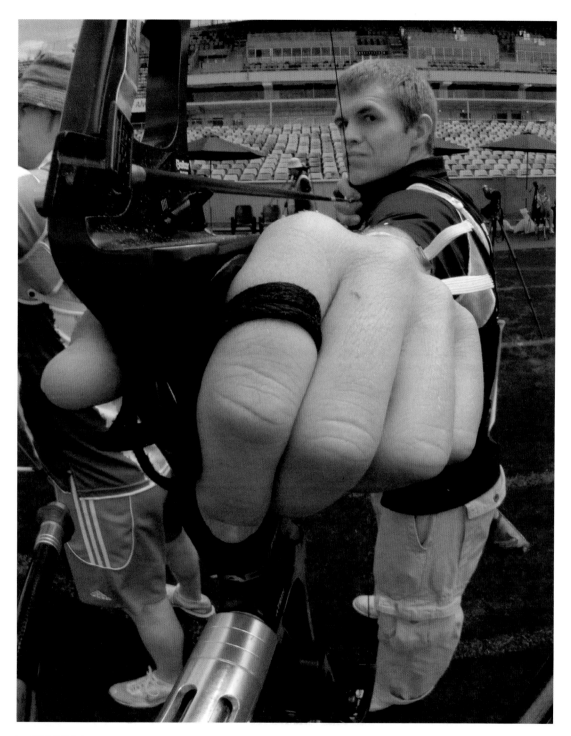

FIGURE 5.4

This is the advised positioning of the bow hand. The index finger rests on the side of the grip, allowing the bow to jump freely forward with no possibility of the fingers to stop it. Also notice how the bow hand thumb is turned out and does not wrap around the bow.

The correct pressure point is easier to maintain when the hand and wrist are bent such that the thumb points straight to the target. Pressure should be directed into and through the thumb to make sure it does not bend. If the thumb begins to wrap around the bow, the pressure point is beginning to be lost. The remedy is to make sure the hand is turning outwards, effectively bending the wrist in a sideways motion. This motion is how the archer should bend the wrist to pull the pinky knuckle back towards himself. Direct the pressure point to the outside of the grip, keeping the pressure point on the base of the thumb, and any unwanted pressure changes to the inside of the hand will cease. Keeping the hand turned out is the hardest part of shooting with a correct grip. As distractions creep in and the pressure point begins to change, the wrist loses the bend and the forward balance of the shot is easily lost. As viewed from the perspective of figure 5.3, the pinky knuckle at the base of the finger needs to remain almost a full centimeter behind the knuckle of the index finger. The bend comes from the wrist; this degree of bend needs to be established, and then maintained, throughout the entire shot.

FIGURE 5.5

This photo shows great bow hand positioning. The knuckles are at a good angle to the riser, the index finger does not sit up high beside the arrow, and the hand looks calm and steady. Notice how the grip fills the entire hand, creating a strong connection with the bow all the way through the hand.

Incorrect positioning

Correct positioning

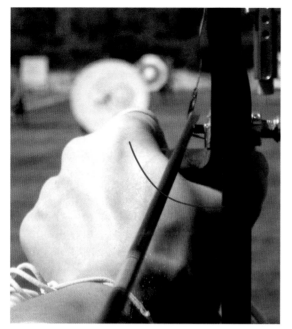

FIGURE 5.6

In the photo on the left, notice how the bow hand forms a definite arc around the bow. The fleshy part of the hand sits well above the riser. Also notice how the entire index finger, and not just the knuckle, is still above the riser. The second picture shows correct positioning with a much flatter bow

hand position in the grip. The index finger knuckle is still above the riser, however the finger points down at the ground and does not wrap around the bow as it does in the first picture. The right picture shows a better directed sense of force through the thumb and into the bow.

Another tip to create a better pressure point is to reach the base of the thumb towards the target such that it makes the thumb become more curved outwards. This outwards curve should be the opposite of wrapping around the bow. Reaching the base of the thumb forward towards the target creates a properly tensioned bow hand, strengthening the connection to the triceps and back muscles. While the base of the thumb is reaching forward, the outer part of the hand curves backwards towards the archer, starting at the base pinky joint. The index finger points downward at the ground. Just as pressure is used to reach the base of the bow hand thumb at the target, the finger should be directed with a small amount of pressure to keep it pointing downward. This pressure keeps the connection throughout the entire bow hand, making for a stronger shot. The main purpose of this is to establish better contact through the throat of the grip and to keep the index finger knuckle from rising too high past the edge of the riser. The fingers of the hand should not be limp like noodles, however they should not be locked solid and tight. The pressure should be consistent throughout the thumb, index, and pinky fingers.

It is a common misconception that all of the pressure should be directed through the pressure point. There must be pressure everywhere on the grip, however there is a bias of pressure on the pressure point. Often archers will emphasize too much pressure on the pressure point, losing the connection with the throat of the grip, and will subsequently lose direction and control of the bow. The throat of the grip is also the vertical pivot point of the bow, doubly increasing the importance of having a strong and balanced kumi, because it is the axis around which any torque will occur.

The steps for placing the hand in the grip are as follows: reach the base of the thumb forward and establish a connection throughout the bow arm, triceps, wrist, hand, and fingers. Reach the bow hand up into the throat of the grip as high as possible. Then find the edge of the grip and push the base of the hand down onto the grip so the lifeline of the hand is just on the edge of the grip. Make sure the index finger maintains its pressure down to the ground and the thumb force points straight toward the target. The hand fills the whole grip with pressure, however there is an emphasis on the pressure point. With all of these steps completed, the archer is ready to come to the set position.

Review

The grip is one of only two places where the archer directly interacts with the bow and is accordingly critical. Like "Hooking," Chapter 4, grip positioning must be consistent from shot to shot and unchanging during each individual shot. Intensity in the bow hand must be used to maintain consistent force and direction of the pressure point through the hand and into the bow, and so the bow hand cannot be too relaxed. A common symptom of a hand that is too relaxed is the string buzzing or slapping the armguard. A totally relaxed bow hand rolls the pressure point in towards the middle of the hand, which in turn exerts pressure on the inward (closer to the body) side of the grip. This force and direction will make the bow jump into the bow arm, making for a weak or even dangerous shot.

The key elements to remember about grip positioning are:

• the hand must first be positioned up into the top of the grip and then settled down until the base of the hand makes contact with the bow

• the pressure point should be at the base of the thumb

• the pinky finger knuckle should be pulled back toward the body as far as possible

• the index finger should point down at the ground to help prepare direction for the bow hand release

• the thumb should hold intensity and point out to the side of the bow much like a hitchhiker's thumb

• the pressure point on the grip should sit on the outside half of the grip so as to project the energy of the bow out and away from the archer such that the string does not hit the bow arm upon release

Grip positioning relates directly to Chapter 19, "Bow Hand Release," which sets the forward force and direction of the bow at the moment of release. Much of the positioning setup while finding correct grip positioning determines how the bow hand will react upon release. Incorrect grip pressure or positioning will throw off the bow hand release and destroy the forward direction of the shot. The difficulty of grip positioning is maintaining the exact pressure point position throughout the entire shot. A lack of strength or focus will change the direction of force, creating errant shots.

Making Bow Grips

Creating a custom bow grip is a rite of passage for an archer. Correct positioning and pressure is impossible without a precisely shaped and angled grip. Much as an archer's finger tab is sized to his hands accordingly, so too must the grip of his bow. It is possible to purchase custom grips from a variety of manufacturers, however one will get the best results if he first makes his own prototype, and then has a professional create a more polished and aesthetically pleasing final product afterward. To begin making a custom grip, purchase a quick setting epoxy or polyester resin/organic peroxide combination that can be mixed and added to the bow's existing grip (plumber's epoxy/putty, Bondo™). These compounds harden quickly (10 minutes - 24 hours) and can be shaped by hand or rasp.

Measure the distance between the web of your hand and the heel – this is the desired length of your new grip. Shorter than this and you may hurt your hand; longer than this and you will lack precise positioning. Refer back to figure 5.2 for guidelines on shape and width of the grip throughout the hand. Most grips are no bigger than 1.5 inches across at their widest.

If viewed perpendicularly to the sight window (as in figure 5.3), the grip's side-profile should be seen as a straight, sloping line. The grip must not have a hump. The vertical angle of the grip is relative to individual archers. If you are struggling with a high bow shoulder, try shooting a lower grip. Higher angled grips tend to be more resistant to bow hand torque, however they are more difficult to shoot and require greater strength. Start out with approximately a 30 or 40 degree angle and go from there.

When viewed from behind the bow (as though from an archer's perspective), the grip should slope flatly from left to right. For a right handed shooter, the left edge of the grip must be slightly higher than the right (at an angle measuring approximately 5 degrees). This angle aids the bow hand wrist by bending it outwards, helping to pull the pinky knuckle back, and positioning the pressure point on the outside (right) half of the grip.

Use a file to smooth out any lumps, pockets, or edges in the material, and make fine-tune adjustments to shape and size.

Many archers wrap their grips with tennis grip wrap. A wrap will aid in comfort and difficulties with sweat buildup. A good grip position is one that feels solid and never changes position. Try multiple brands of tape and decide which one works best.

ULTIMA

MAKING BOW GRIPS

6 Head Position

Head position is the placement, twist, and elevation of the head while shooting. Head positioning may seem simple, but it is an exercise of control that archers continually must struggle with to execute with precision.

It is one of the final elements of his technique that an archer will master. After hooking the string, placing one's hand in the grip, and aligning his shoulders at the target, the archer should turn his head full-on to the target, addressing it with his eyes and all of his consciousness, and then never move the head from this position. Through much practice, the archer must learn how to allow all of his individual body parts to move independently of one another.

For many archers, head position changes as the arms raise to the target and begin the drawing motions. For others, the slight discomfort of finding the anchor position causes a slight change in head position. Even one centimeter, in any direction, is far too much movement as many top archers will spend months trying to eliminate movements measured by mere millimeters. The head must be able to swivel to the target without pulling the shoulders out of alignment. Then as the archer begins to draw, the powerful turning of the shoulders must not cause involuntary twisting or tilting of the head. The head must be an island, unaffected by the power moving below.

Part of what makes head positioning so difficult is the fact that the head has many degrees of freedom. It can twist left and right, nod up and down, push forward and backward, and tilt from side to side. The archer's head often likes to do all of these things at the same time. Each of these directions of motion must be examined and dealt with as the archer finds his optimal head position and then builds experience holding it.

FIGURE 6.1

Here is an archer with a comfortable and natural head position. The chin is slightly elevated while the entire head is turned as far as possible in the direction of the target. The slight bias of lean toward the draw hand side creates more relaxed neck muscles, resulting in better holding energies.

Incorrect head position tilted toward archer's bow shoulder

Correct head position biased to archer's dominant hand

FIGURE 6.2

Notice a key difference in the intensity of the eyes between the two photos. In the incorrect photo the eyes look anxious, strained, and stressed. In the more relaxed head position, see how even the eyes are able to comfortably focus on their aiming point.

After hooking and finding the grip position, the archer should turn his face and eyes to the target. The head should be turned so far that the edge of the chin should be overtop of the bow shoulder. Generally, the farther the archer can comfortably turn his head to face the target, the greater the connection he can achieve with the back muscles. Do not become discouraged! A beginning archer will need to stretch his neck considerably to achieve this degree of rotation. Three weeks of very consistent and determined stretching may be needed before the requisite rotation can be comfortably achieved. As long as the head does not tilt toward the bow shoulder, it is almost impossible to rotate too far to the target. These motions happen either while or just after the shoulders also turn to the target. Thus we find ourselves in the set position. Read Chapter 8, "Set Position," concomitantly with this chapter for the greatest clarification on positioning. The archer cannot start raising the bow to the target until the eyes have settled on the aiming point (see Chapter 26, "Eye Focus"), and the face is completely rotated to address the target. Take a moment at the set position to complete this step – many archers will ruin a shot before it has begun by raising the bow without fully addressing the target with their face. Remain there for a full second while training, and slowly decrease that time to around half-a-second after considerable practice. The pause will allow the body to settle, feel the direction of the target, and allow the mindset of the archer to switch into shooting mode. Without this shifting of mindset or final addressing of the target with the face, the archer will become lost in the shot and lose connection with the bow.

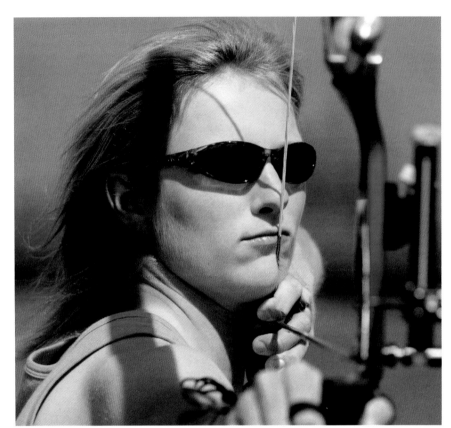

FIGURE 6.3

In this photo, notice the amount of head rotation towards the target (in this case, the camera). The right edge of her chin (the archer's right), is almost rotated so much that it overlaps part of the deltoid of her draw shoulder. Archers must be able to achieve at least this much rotation. More rotation is better, provided the archer is still relaxed and is not straining too much.

The eyes must be level or tilted just slightly in the direction of the archer's dominant hand. For right handed archers, a tiny tilt to the right is acceptable – the archer's right. Any tilting to the left is absolutely detrimental, and the archer will begin to lose connection with his stomach and core, his main source of power. For left handed archers, the opposite is true. A slight bias toward the archer's dominant hand allows the sternomastoid (see figure 6.4), the large muscle running up the side of the neck, to relax just a bit more, which makes anchoring, transfer, holding, and expansion easier. The most subtle changes in position have very significant affects on the outcome of shooting. See figure 6.2 for before and after photos of an archer showing slight changes in head tilt.

An ideal head position makes the archer feel as if he is slightly peering down his nose as he looks at the target. The chin is raised up; the chin is not tucked toward the throat. Think of it as holding one's head high, but not so high that the nose reaches an unfriendly level. Others have imagined it as thinking they were royalty. It is an exalted position. By barely lifting the chin, the archer opens up the throat, allowing for an easier and more comfortable anchor. Elevate the line of the jaw so it is closer to parallel with the ground, allowing the archer to make contact along the entire hand and thumb with his anchor. See figure 13.4, featuring details of the positioning.

Imagine the archer has a string attached to the very top of his head that is pulling easily and gently upward. The point here is that the neck should be relaxed and tall. The neck should not be compressed and tight. With the head sitting high and light, it is easier to achieve greater amounts of rotation toward the target.

Lengthen the neck, pressing the chin forward as much as possible, within reason, to give the archer greater room under the jaw for anchoring. If the archer does the opposite and pulls the chin back to the throat, the muscles of the neck become much tighter and do not allow the head to move independently of the shoulders. A slight push forward, like a chicken pushing its head forward as it struts around, also helps the archer achieve more consistent clicker positioning by giving an absolute position for the head. By giving the head maximized direction and end control in one of its degrees of freedom, archers can minimize movement. An archer commonly struggles if he moves his head either forward or back as he tries to accommodate a greater draw length. Instead, to move the head position forward is better, forcing the archer to draw more angularly and through the body to achieve the loading position (Chapter 12).

FIGURE 6.4

The sternomastoid, indicated by the red arrow, serves as a pocket for the anchor position, (see Chapter 13), and control the side-to-side tilt of the head position. Notice how the drawing hand thumb comes into contact with the sternomastoid while the bowstring contacts the jaw at the loading position. At the anchor position all gaps are closed. By keeping the shoulders down and leaning the head slightly toward the drawing side, it should remain relaxed while shooting. Atypical archers with outstanding flexibility and extra long fingers are capable of hooking their drawing thumb behind the sternomastoid at the loading and anchor position for even greater alignment at full draw.

Drawing   **Loading position**   **Anchor position**

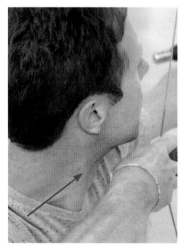
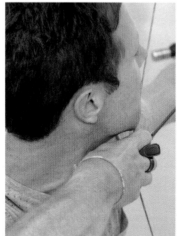
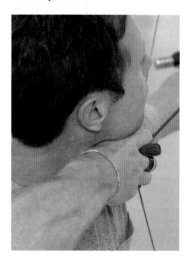

6 HEAD POSITION

FIGURE 6.5

Here we see an archer wearing sunglasses and using a comfortable head position. Notice the slight bias to the drawing-side hand.

Sunglasses may be a helpful tool for archers shooting outdoors. The obvious benefit of relaxing the eyes and blocking glare notwithstanding, sunglasses also help an archer with head positioning because they give a frame of reference of rotation, tilt, and elevation. The archer should use either the edge of the glass or the frame of the glasses to reproduce consistent head positioning shot after shot. Slight changes in head positioning become noticeable as the edge of the glass will creep closer to the target, raise or lower in the frame, or something similar. While many archers feel as though they cannot turn their head enough to the target to use sunglasses, if they stretch on a regular basis and go through the processes described in these chapters, nearly every archer will be able to achieve enough rotation to use sunglasses.

Review

Head positioning helps control aiming and eye focus, Chapters 23 and 26, and provides consistent positioning for the anchor, Chapter 13. The head position is also related to "Posture," Chapter 2, as small changes in head position can drastically affect the curvature of the spine and the position of the head relative to the shoulders or hips. In fact, the head tends to be a first mover – a small tendency in the head to move will be noticed as a larger movement or instability in the rest of the body. Focus on achieving correct head positioning with zero movement throughout the shot and the rest of the posture will follow.

The key elements to remember about head positioning are:

• a line drawn across the eyebrows should lean slightly towards the string hand side

• the head should be rotated so much that the edge of the chin should sit overtop the edge of the drawing shoulder

• the head should remain absolutely still throughout the entire shot

• a line drawn to the ground from the string's point of contact on the chin should not touch the chest or hips; if it does, the head is not out enough or is under rotated

• viewed from directly behind the archer's drawing elbow, or in front of the archer, viewed from under the line of the arrow, the head should occupy the farthest outward position away from the body

• the chin should be elevated such that the archer is slightly peering down his nose

• a high head position helps the neck be as flexible as possible. To achieve this, imagine as though a string is pulling the head upwards, elongating the neck

The head position is a controlling feature for many other elements of the shot. A slight change in head position can even affect the amount of fear an archer expresses on his face. A litany of small problems are often corrected by focusing on achieving correct head position and maintaining it. As the head can twist, tilt, jut in and out, and elevate, keeping the head completely still throughout the entire shot is not a trivial task.

7 Bow Arm

The bow arm reaches to the target and provides the forward stabilization for the shot.

Think about the bow arm as a bridge truss: solid, strong, and braced by a powerful foundation. As with all the other positions in archery, the foundation and source of intensity for the bow arm comes from the body's core. The bow arm must be positioned so it can tap into the core's power, allowing the archer to aim with his entire body. The arm shakes and quivers under load, but the body holds strong. The bow arm is not a separate entity; it is an extension of the core energy of the body.

The first time to think about the bow arm is after hooking the string, and after positioning the bow hand in the grip – just before thinking about the set position. The archer must begin to attain the set position by pushing his bow arm straight, rotating the elbow down, and extending the shoulder position forward. When the set position is finally achieved, the bow arm should be pointed down at the ground at approximately a 45 degree angle. The arm should extend forward, along this 45 degree angle line (see figure 7.1). The archer should not achieve proper shoulder extension by rolling the shoulder forward, but by imagining someone is holding something just beyond the reach of his bow arm and he must reach to try and touch it. Body positioning must remain absolutely still while attempting this reach. It is common to feel a stretch across the top of the deltoid muscle. Beginners of this technique will definitely feel a stretch – if they do not, they are not reaching far enough. The arm should be reached until it is straight and taut, though not shaking with exertion. In the past, archers have been taught to hold the bow arm scapula back and down, however doing so creates a limited range of motion, or possible impingement, for angular drawing and expansion. Reaching the bow arm forward until taut and connected creates the necessary space while still providing the most stable and repeatable position.

FIGURE 7.1

Setting the bow arm happens at the set position, where this photo was taken. By pushing down and out, but directed toward the target, this archer is able to keep a low, stable bow shoulder as she prepares to scoop the arm up at the target.

FIGURE 7.2

Here we see the three main elements of the bow arm: the V created at the shoulder joint, the intense focus on keeping the triceps muscle tight as indicated with the yellow shape and the red circle, (the red circle is where the greatest intensity must be held), and the forward positioning of the scapula. The arrow, as represented by the yellow line, should also be visible at least this amount above the bow shoulder. If the arrow is not visible, the shoulder is too high.

With complete beginners in archery, successful rotation of the bow arm elbow will be the sole predictor of an enjoyable first day. A lack of elbow rotation nearly guarantees the archer will hit his arm with the string. Advanced archers, of course, are subject to the same physics, and must check their bow arm elbow rotation every single shot lest they slip up and create a painful and unsightly blemish. The bow arm must be fully rotated, at least until the bony parts of the elbow line up vertically, pointing down at the ground. Losing sufficient rotation while drawing, holding, or expanding is easy, and the tiniest loss will result in a collapsing shot or a painful slap from the string. To help maintain the elbow rotation, push more with the bow arm and keep a strong pressure point in the grip. As in Chapter 5, "Grip Positioning," pulling the pinky knuckle back and keeping good index finger positioning will also help with maintaining the elbow rotation. The pinky knuckle should be pulled back far enough that muscles on the top of the forearm bulge with intensity.

FIGURE 7.3

The red line shows the elbow rotation. The bony protrusions of the elbow joint where the radius and the ulna join must align as shown by the yellow arrow. The red arrow shows the direction of rotation. Holding a strong triceps muscle will help maintain this rotation and provide direction for the bow arm.

Direction is very important for the bow arm. The direction comes mostly from the shoulder. To imagine that the arm stops at the shoulder and the rest of it is dead, immovable, can help the archer to learn to use the body to provide direction and control of the entire bow arm, rather than using its smaller muscles. At the set position, the forward direction of the bow shoulder should point in the same direction as the target. This is all part of addressing the target and minimizing excess motion when raising the bow. If the body must twist even more when raising on the target to achieve the correct shoulder alignment, the bow arm direction has not been set properly. The entire body must feel the direction at the target.

The key focal point of the bow arm for maintaining its intensity and power is the triceps muscle. The triceps muscle is the one that burns from doing push-ups. See the archer in figure 7.2 and his bulging triceps muscle, resisting the force of the bow. There is no trick, one simply must hold the intensity in the triceps. Upon release, intensity must be maintained even still, otherwise the bow hand release will not properly snap forward and the bow arm will drop. See Chapter 19, "Bow Hand Release," for discussions on this topic. The bow arm must maintain its force and direction past the follow-through position.

To maintain the forward reach of the bow arm upon raising at the target, one should imagine scooping his arm forward and out, while raising at the same time. The archer needs to keep a consistent pressure point, using it as the focal point of the scooping motion. For a detailed discussion on raising the bow at the target, see the second part of Chapter 8, "Set Position," that deals with raising the bow. Correct eye focus will help, but the archer needs to make sure correct direction is maintained throughout the entire shot. After being raised above the target bale, the bow should settle down toward the center of target. While the bow arm settles a small amount of breath is exhaled, allowing the chest to stay down and the bow arm position to reset itself down and out again (more on breathing and rhythm in Chapter 22). During this settling, a "V" should be created by the archer's bow shoulder. Recall Chapter 5, "Grip Positioning," and see Chapter 9, "Setup Position," for more discussions on the V of the bow arm shoulder. It is an active motion to recheck the bow arm positioning down and out, and should be seen as a specific step prior to reaching the setup position. Figure 7.5 shows a stop-frame example of resetting the bow arm while coming to the setup position.

FIGURE 7.4

This archer doing a strength drill (his 50 pound draw weight plus a 15 pound stretch band) uses great bow arm rotation and shoulder positioning to create a strong foundation for the shot. Notice how his elbow is rotated down and out while the bow arm shoulder reaches toward the direction of the target.

Bow arm shoulder height before setting   **Bow arm shoulder height after setting**

FIGURE 7.5

These two pictures show an archer setting his bow arm shoulder down and forward as he comes to the setup position. The red line represents the bow arm shoulder height in the left photo, while the yellow line represents the bow arm shoulder height in the right photo. The lines are drawn from the divot in the archer's shoulder. To achieve this setting of the shoulder, the archer is actually reaching upwards with his bow hand, while reaching forward to the target through his bow arm shoulder. The result is a setting down and forward of the bow arm shoulder position, locking it into place for the rest of the shot. Complete the motion depicted here rather than relying completely on setting the bow arm shoulder at the set position – it is very difficult to set the shoulder low and keep it low while raising the bow at the target. By resetting the bow arm shoulder while coming to the setup position, it is easier to be more consistent, stronger, and more confident.

Upon release, the shoulder alignment at the target must be maintained by keeping a strong triceps muscle. Nearly all weak shots are created by a weak bow arm. There is more mental energy in hooking the string and drawing, and it is typically done by the archer's dominant hand, hence also having more control over the archer's brain. Everyone spends so much time working on their release or coming off the string as fast as possible. However, to produce the desired effect, these archers should pay more attention to the bow arm. Maintaining the triceps strength and projecting the force of the bow forward through the pressure point will create the desired sharp, cutting release.

Review

A solid bow arm works in conjunction with "Grip Positioning," Chapter 5, and the "Bow Hand Release," Chapter 19, to create the forward balance of each shot. Fixing the bow arm is a component of "Set Position," as discussed in the following chapter. Most archers are so concerned with the movement of the draw and are focused on having a good release off the string they forget the forward half of the shot completely! A great majority of weak shots are caused by inattention and weakness or breaking in the bow arm intensity. The brain must manage two opposing forces without interruption to either, (forward at the target, and angular off the string), despite a signal to relax the fingers of the string hand. A strong bow arm is created by using the whole of the body as a brace, directing intensity down the bow arm and toward the target. The mind's intensity and focus must be directed at the target.

The key elements to remember about the bow arm are:

• forward reach at the target

• beginners to this technique will feel a stretching sensation forward and through the shoulder joint and upper deltoid

• intensity must be doubly maintained through the shot – through the bow hand release, and long after the follow through

• rotating the elbow down will help with string clearance and allow for better intensity control of the triceps muscle

• the intensity of the triceps muscle connects the power of the bow arm shoulder with the rest of the body

• as the bow is settled down to the target after raising above it, the bow arm must be smoothly, yet forcefully, extended down and out as far as possible towards the target

A lot of feel is used with the bow arm. The feeling of intensity and strength from the lower abdomen must be directed through the bow arm. The bow arm must reach as far as possible toward the target, allowing the archer to feel as though he is inside the bow (see Chapter 16, "Holding," for further clarification on being inside the bow). Posture (Chapter 2) can greatly affect the bow arm, as leaning over the toes, the heels, or either the right or left leg will throw off the balance of the shot and disconnect the archer from the feeling of power of being inside the bow.

AGGHH!! I'M GOING CRAZY!

Archery can be the most maddening task on the planet. And what makes it worse, there are countless people, books, and literature that claim you must shoot archery relaxed, calm, and controlled. "Calm?! Controlled?! Relaxed?! Are you out of your mind?! You want me to do what with my shoulder?!" We've all been there. Truth is, we probably are still there. Golfers likely sympathize because golf has a similar balance of control, precision, and impossibility that leads quickly to bomb sized frustration. Then, in the midst of making technique changes, athletes must compete now too? This clearly is not the recipe for happiness and success.

Desire is very powerful. It is our desire for perfection, for that 60, the personal best, heck, even just one comfortably shot arrow, that sends our emotions spiraling out of control. Some might argue that you can learn to control your desire, but on closer examination it all seems relative. What archer in the gold medal final of the Olympics was not wishing with every fiber of his being that he could just hold it together for 12 more arrows. "Just 12 more, and then you can go crazy."

The thing is, it is that same inner voice that says, "Just 12 more," that also says, "I can't do this. I'm not strong enough. I'm not good enough." But most importantly, it is that same voice that sounds the death knell, "Just quit!" In those moments when it hurts the most, remember standing on your favorite practice field. Perhaps you have friends around you, or perhaps you are by yourself enjoying the sun fading over the hills. Remember the sound of the bowstring and the satisfying dull thud of your arrow landing in the middle of the target. Remember that feeling. Remember the quiet happiness in your heart.

Nothing hurts more than months and months of maddeningly frustrating hard work, and then losing at the big competition. The quiver often feels like it weighs 1000 pounds when you slip it off of your hips. It's OK – you can do it. Just keep on trying. It's worth it.

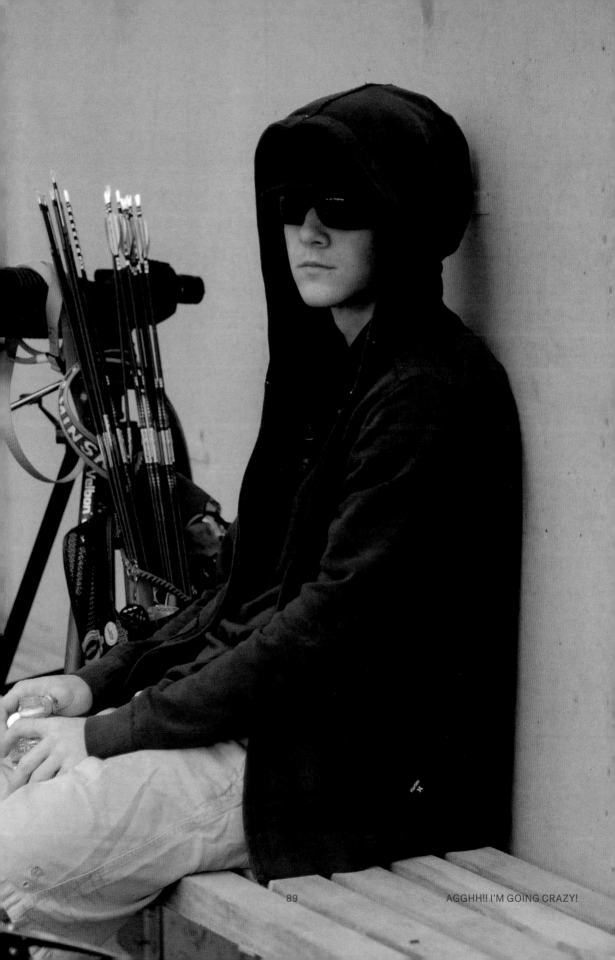

AGGHH!! I'M GOING CRAZY!

8   Set Position

Set position is the ready position the archer assumes after setting the proper hook on the string and the correct hand placement in the grip.

Not to be confused with the setup position (discussed in the next chapter), set position occurs before the archer begins to raise the bow to the target. Set position is essentially a final readying and checking of the body after setting the feet, balance, trunk twist, hooking, and gripping. There are a few final preparations made in the set position that make it so critical: set position is where the archer first establishes his shoulder alignment and where head positioning, one of the most critical elements of the shot, is locked into place.

To achieve the set position, the archer must first turn his head all the way to the final head position. Archers should not move their heads from this original set, so getting it right is of paramount importance for the rest of the shot. Immediately after setting head position (or concurrently, if the archer is truly able to do both without sacrificing either), twist the torso such that the hips stay in their open position, relatively 20-25 degrees open to the target, so that the shoulder alignment is directed at the target. Realize the draw hand and wrist remain unchanged, as they are connected to the string the entire time. Of utmost importance: the hand positions on the grip of the bow and the position of the fingers hooking the string do not change the tiniest amount during these steps, or during any step for that matter. See Chapter 5, "Grip Positioning," and Chapter 4, "Hooking," for more information and reminders. At this stage of set position, only head positioning and shoulder alignment have been established. Remember that head and shoulder alignment can be achieved with bent arms – a straight bow arm is not yet needed, and, in fact, it is easier for people to check string hooking and grip positioning with a bent bow arm such that it brings the bow hand up around stomach level.

Checking hooking and grip position with bent bow arm

Preparing to straighten bow arm and fully address target

Final set position with raised head

FIGURE 8.1

See how the power of the archer's posture changes between each of the photos despite there being very minimal changes in physical positioning. In the last photo notice how far forward the drawing elbow position is and how tight the biceps is to the pectoral muscle. The archer is already 'inside the bow' by using the structure of his body to resist the force of the string.

FIGURE 8.2

Notice how the positioning of the draw hand elbow is forward of perpendicular to the archer. This creates an obtuse angle between the upper arm, which is pulled tight against the chest by the back muscles and the forearm. Also notice the pushed down and out bow arm shoulder, reaching toward the target. The energy of the bow shoulder is directed into the grip through the bow hand pressure point while the bow arm elbow is rotated downwards while maintaining the connection throughout the arm and pressure point. Fight the tendency to raise the bow by raising the shoulders, instead raise with the top finger string hook, bow hand pressure point, and balanced back muscles. Lastly, note the calm and relaxed head position. The chin is up such that the jaw is near parallel with the ground, the neck is long, and the head is biased slightly toward the drawing side. Also, the head is rotated far towards the target.

After achieving head positioning and shoulder alignment, keep the front shoulder in place, and push the bow arm until the elbow is no longer bent. In order to keep the rear shoulder positioning as well, the lower trapezius muscle must be activated and held. Pushing the bow arm straight means the drawing arm reaches with it across the chest. The biceps muscle should be relaxed, but it must sit flush and squeeze into the pectoral muscle. Imagine the archer would hold a pencil between his chest and the biceps muscle – this is the squeezing sensation. The string will be drawn only a few inches from its brace height setting. If the archer is drawing the string such that the arrow is drawn more than 4 or 5 inches, he is most likely not achieving set positioning. The set position is more of an internal twisting and compressing: a readying of the body to control the power of drawing.

FIGURE 8.3

Though this archer does not rotate his shoulders as much to the target prior to lifting the bow, he still is in a good set position due to his low and forward bow arm positioning and his relaxed drawing hand. As he starts to pick up the bow and move to the setup position, he will turn his shoulders slightly, achieving the 'inside the bow' concept that is often talked about in this book.

Archers should feel very relaxed in set position. The power of the body is held low and deep in the abdomen, leaving the head and shoulders free to easily rotate to the necessary positions. The goal of the set position is to ready the body for drawing by establishing correct shoulder and head positions with the lowest possible energy state to hold those positions. Generally, beginning archers will use far too much power and motion to get to the set position. One should try to minimize motion and movement making set position the most energy efficient position.

Drawing elbow position is an often misunderstood point, though it defines the set position. If viewed from the side (as in figures 8.1 and 8.2), the elbow should be as far forward of perpendicular as possible, while still maintaining correct shoulder alignment and elevation. By keeping the elbow forward while using the upper arm to counterbalance the chest with the holding force of the back muscles, the archer is able to engage more of the back muscles. Failing to keep the rear shoulder down as the draw hand and elbow come across the chest can quickly lead to impingement injuries.

Here is one of the few elements of technique described in this book that requires an extra word to equate gender difference: it is critical that the female archer first reaches up and over the breast before getting to the set position. Lifting the arm over the breast should not elevate or bind the shoulder position. This will ensure there is no obstruction for raising the bow at the target and will allow the female archer to be able to reach forward far enough to achieve the correct set position. This clarification is only for potential difficulties – it is not required if obstruction is not an issue.

The jaw-line angle is an often overlooked element of head positioning. As archers tend to look down at their bow hands and string hooking, they also tend to leave their heads looking down when they get to set position. The archer then has no direction to the target if he starts to raise the bow before completely addressing the target with his face. Anchoring becomes more difficult with the resulting downward head position because there is less room under the jaw. The muscle running up the side of the neck is also generally more tense. The secret is to raise the chin up at the set position such that the archer feels as though he is peering down over his nose (like royalty, see Chapter 6). While the head position feels pronouncedly raised because the arms are still down, once raised up to the target the head position will feel more natural. Again, the focus is to establish head position once, at set position, for the entire shot and never move it from the position established. In order for the archer to accomplish set position, it is imperative that he performs each of the following: sets the hips, the shoulders, string hooking, grip positioning, turns and raises the head, straightens the bow arm, and realizes the set position. There should be a slight pause of half a second or so as the archer controls the motion, balances the forces of the body, and addresses the target. Only then can the archer begin to raise the bow with direction and clarity of motion.

FIGURE 8.4

Here we see an archer arriving at the set position after first checking string hooking in the picture on the left, and setting the grip pressure point while balancing the load with his back in the picture on the right. The bow arm projects down at approximately a 45 degree angle. Notice how the bowarm goes from bent to straight.

FIGURE 8.5

For a bad example, look at this photo showing an archer at a set position that is too far back. His drawing elbow is almost a 90 degree angle with his shoulder, and he is pulling the string back much too far. Contrast this photo with figure 8.2 and observe these two differences of position.

FIGURE 8.6

Here we can see the twisting of the bow as the archer raises it above the target and begins drawing. In the first photo the archer is just starting the drawing motion after raising the bow to its highest position over the target. The arrow and stabilizer clearly point toward the left side of the photo. In the middle photo (the archer is almost at the loading position), notice how the bow arm and hand position has not noticeably moved left to right, however the stabilizer and arrow now must point more along the archer's line of force at the target (his bow arm). This means that during angular drawing, the bow rotates in the archer's hand until it comes into alignment with his force direction. In the last photo we can see the archer's bow arm and the stabilizer now point is almost the same direction. This is perfect positioning.

Raising the Bow

After the set position but before the setup position, the archer raises his bow at the target. The techniques for the bow arm described in Chapter 7 are important to raising the bow, as are those Chapter 9, "Setup Position." The main concern of raising the bow at the target is not the muscles used to do so, but that the motion is accomplished with the muscles remaining set, and so raising the bow is a continuation of set position. Setup position will come after the bow has been raised with the technique elements achieved at set position entirely intact.

The correct way to raise the bow at the target is not to simply raise the bow straight up through the target with the bow held pointing in the same direction, but instead to raise up to the side to maintain shoulder alignment, while allowing the bow to rotate in your hand from angular drawing. See Figure 8.6 as a good example of the bow rotating in the archer's hands, and that such a motion would make the sight pin move from left to right across the target face for a right handed archer. It is only at the loading position that the bow ultimately points towards the target – during set, setup, and drawing, the bow should not be straight or level, and instead should move in an arc to go along with angular drawing. Angular drawing becomes easier when the shoulders are not completely bound up in forced positions. Lifting the bow around the side and settling down onto the target, and more importantly, settling down into and inside the body, will make the movements from set, to setup, with angular drawing to loading, holding, and expansion, easier and more fluid. Biomechanically, movements in arcs are better than straight lines because of how our bodies are formed. The important arcing movement is depicted in figures 8.6, 8.7, 8.8, 8.9 and 9.6, which show the sight moving across the target face and settling down onto the target as the bow rotates in the shooter's hand. Aiming is not yet required and should not yet concern the archer. The archer's concern, at present, is the direction and orientation of the bow. As the archer approaches the loading position, his motions should result in the sight being close to the aiming point. The eyes should only be focused on the aiming point and should never pay direct attention to the sight. Nor should the archer ever think, "I need to start drawing when my sight is in the two-ring," or something similar. Figure 8.7 merely outlines a shape for the movement, represents approximates, and uses the sight to provide a visual aide to teach the correct motions. Remember that while the sight is moving from left to right, the bow is also rotating! The bow arm position should not change, and thus the sight should settle either on the aiming point or very near the aiming point. Take care that the sight never drops below the aiming points and the archer has to come back up the target face to begin aiming and expansion.

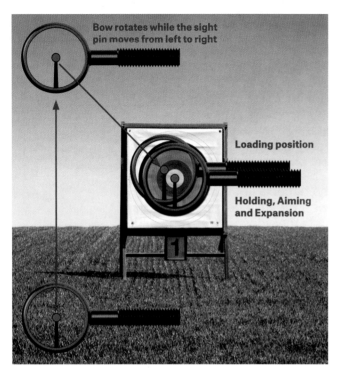

Bow rotates while the sight pin moves from left to right

Loading position

Holding, Aiming and Expansion

FIGURE 8.7

The strongest and most fluid way of raising the bow at the target is to reach towards the target with the bow arm, while allowing the bow to point off to the side. Once moving through the setup position and using angular drawing motions to get to the holding position, the bow will naturally rotate and change the relative position of the sight pin on the target as the arms come closer to the body center-line at the loading position. Notice how the bow points well above the target at its highest point, though the relative distances above or to the side of the target do not matter so much. Do not watch the sight pin while raising the bow!

From the highest point above the target, the bow should move from left to right, coming back to the target while the drawing arm is moving angularly towards the loading position. This left to right motion of the sight pin is from the bow rotating, as shown in figures 8.6, 8.8, and 9.6.

FIGURE 8.8

In these three pictures we can see the red line, depicting the string, moving from outside the target (to the archer's right) inwards and closer to the archer's body as she lifts the bow and draws it. The yellow arrow represents the direction and orientation of the bow. The red, yellow and green shapes show the shoulder positions of each step and how much they change during the movement. Notice clearly how the shapes move near horizontally to the left.

From this rear view, this is what angular motion would look like as the archer brings the bow closer to her body while raising and drawing the bow. The green line at the bottom shows that her body is maintaining position and is not rotating or leaning backwards. The extreme differences between the red, yellow and green shapes in the last picture are purely a result of the archer rotating her shoulder around, not by her leaning or changing her posture.

FIGURE 8.9

Here we can see an archer going through a progression of raising his bow at the target, coming to the setup position, drawing, arriving at the loading position, and anchoring. Notice how much drawing shoulder rotation he achieves between each of the positions, especially from frames 1 to 5. In the second frame we can see the archer starting to rotate his shoulder – in his view the sight pin moves from left to right and down to the target as shown by figure 8.7. The third frame is the highest point of raising the bow at the target. The archer comes to the setup position just one moment later. Frame 3 represents the shoulder motion that occurs immediately as drawing starts, and frame 4 represents about a tenth of a second into drawing. Notice the gap between the archer's drawing biceps muscle and his ear as the forearm is elevated relative to the upper arm and deltoid. We can clearly see a settling of the drawing shoulder as it moves down and around to draw the bow. Lastly, notice the twisting orientation of the bow between all of the frames. Notice how the stabilizer begins to move from left to right as the bow twists in the archer's hand. This is especially obvious as he starts to draw the bow between frames 2 through 5. This matches with figures 8.6, 8.7, 8.8, and 9.6. Don't worry about keeping the bow perfectly vertical during raising and drawing so long as it reaches vertical at the loading and anchor positions.

When first starting to raise the bow, it is the thumb of the grip hand that provides the most direction and feeling. The thumb beginning its arc to the right of the riser already helps to provide direction for the bow arm. By thinking about moving the taut thumb, and, consequently, the pressure point in the grip hand, along the path depicted in figure 8.7, the rest of the arm will follow along.

As angular drawing is an outside to inside motion (the drawing shoulder starts at a forward and out position, rotating around during drawing to bring the drawing hand into the body), it makes sense that similar motion should be embraced throughout the entire shot. The goal of shooting with angular energies is to bring the hands, arms, and shoulders more inside the body, such that greater connections are made and more power can be used to hold the bow as still as possible. Starting the angular motion of the drawing shoulder in the upper half of raising the bow at the target helps start the angular energies of drawing sooner and creates more fluidity and control to the shot. It is of utmost importance that the arm and wrist positions established at hooking and at the set position remain as they are, and that any movement of the arms closer to the body as the archer brings the bow into alignment with the target are only produced by rotation of the drawing shoulder. If any wrist bend or lateral movement of the drawing elbow occurs, a disconnection occurs. Remember, these potential errors of motion are very subtle, and they will only be noticed by the keenest of eyes or by someone who is watching for them specifically.

FIGURE 8.10

This picture addresses a common misunderstanding that imagines the bow must point directly at the target while at the set position. The long yellow line shows the direction toward the target, which is parallel with the forward force of the front shoulder. The red line points the same direction as the arrow, indicating the cocked position of the bow, though the direction of the archer's attention is along the yellow lines. The reason the alignment must look like this at the set position is because the archer will face impingement problems while raising the bow if the red and yellow lines both point at the target. After raising the bow at the target he will bring the bow into direction alignment while drawing. This motion is the strongest and most fluid way to draw a bow.

Review

The set position is an important readying position. It is the final moment of stillness prior to raising the bow at the target and shooting. Once movement is initiated it must not be stopped. Thus, the set position is where absolute conviction must be created. Coming to the set position must look calm and natural. There should be very little motion as all of the intensity should be in directional control.

The key elements to remember about the set position are:

• the bow arm presses forward and downward toward the target at an approximate 45 degree angle

• the drawing arm should reach forward, across the chest

• the hooking position must remain exactly the same while coming to the set position

• the goal of the set position is to prepare the body with directional intensity control with as little movement as possible

• the bow, when being raised at the target, should first swoop out around and to the side in an arcing fashion, and then settle down onto the target

• as the bow is settled down to the target after raising above it, the bow arm must be smoothly, yet forcefully, extended down and out as far as possible towards the target (see figure 7.5 for more clarification)

• while the bow is being raised, and especially as it begins to settle towards the target, the drawing shoulder must use the directional intensity established at the set position to ensure that drawing the bow is done completely angularly

The set position connects many technique elements, namely hooking (Chapter 4), grip positioning (Chapter 5), and head position (Chapter 6). It prepares the body for angular drawing, Chapters 10 and 11, and, eventually, for holding and release, Chapters 16 and 18. The archer brings all formerly completed technique elements into the set position, the final readying for the larger movements of shooting to follow.

9   Setup Position

The setup position, the prepared position with the bow raised at the target, ready to be drawn, gives the archer the last sense of direction prior to drawing the bow and completing the shot.

The setup position occurs after the set position, and the two are separated by the raising of the bow. For many archers, the setup position appears almost skipped because they have a smooth, fluid raise of the bow conjoined with angular drawing of the bow string. Few archers actually have a pause at the setup position like most do at the set position. However, all archers go through the setup position, using it as the starting point of angular motion and the final checkpoint to ensure everything is prepared to execute the shot.

Start by examining figure 9.1 showing an archer pausing at the setup position. All of the key points of the set position – head positioning, angular holding of the back, of the bow arm, and of the grip hand pressure point – have been maintained while raising at the target. The setup position is differentiated from the set position because it gives primary direction for drawing the bow. It is of utmost importance that the LAN 2 is the first body part to move with the drawing motion, not the elbow, and definitely not the drawing hand. This point cannot be stressed enough because if the archer does not start with angular drawing, he will never be able to fully come back to it later.

FIGURE 9.1

Setup position achieved, this archer is now ready to draw the bow. See how the drawing elbow is forward of the drawing shoulder, helping to compress the muscles of the back to give the proper angular direction for drawing. The biceps muscle is squeezing against the chest as though holding a pencil in the crook of the armpit. Note that this particular archer has a slightly low setup position. A more generally accepted positioning would have his drawing wrist at approximately the same elevation as his nose. The setup position should be absolutely no lower than is pictured here.

FIGURE 9.2

The red V depicted in this diagram is the shoulder positioning is created when the bow arm is extended forward, towards the target.

The job of the setup position is to ensure the body is in the correct alignment to give the LAN 2 its direction to draw the bow. The LAN 2 is an area on the back side of the drawing arm and shoulder, not a specific body part. Its role is to serve as a focal point for archers as they angularly draw the bow. It is only possible to move the LAN 2. One cannot hold intensity in it, squeeze it, or clench it. See figures 9.1, 11.2, and 11.4 for images of the LAN 2. Figures 8.8 and 8.9 show stop-action motion of the LAN 2.

After raising the bow to the target, just before reaching the setup position, the bow arm should do a rechecking of its position by pushing down and outwards to ensure a solid connection. Rechecking the bow arm shoulder is important because it is easy to pick up the shoulder just slightly while raising at the target. See figures 7.4, 7.5, and the corresponding segment of the chapter "Bow Arm" between these examples of this technique. If the shoulder starts barely higher than desired, it will only rise even higher when the bow is drawn, or during expansion, resulting in a breaking of the shot. At the set position, the bow arm should reach to the target until a stretch is felt across the top of the deltoid and a deep V is seen in the shoulder. See figures 7.2 and 9.2 for examples of the V.

FIGURE 9.3

These two archers demonstrate good setup positions. In the left photo, notice how the drawing elbow position is forward of the line of the shoulder as indicated by the lines on the picture. This is the key to the setup position because it sets the body up in the correct positioning for angular drawing. In the right photo, notice how the drawing wrist is higher than the elbow and is approximately level with the nose.

At the setup position the drawing hand must be no higher than the nose, or else it will be impossible to retain holding with the low trapezius muscle. The drawing wrist should have the same bent-outward position established at hooking. Not only should the wrist be bent outwards, but it should be bent upwards as well, so that the wrist serves as the highest point that keeps the elbow pulling angularly around the head. If seen from behind the archer, the elbow should almost be in alignment with the arrow, with the wrist outside the line. The principles of hooking upward with correct finger placement, together with the outward wrist position proscribe the rotational relationship of wrist/forearm/elbow. The biceps muscle of the drawing arm should still be pressing against the chest as though holding a pencil in the crook of the shoulder. In this position, the drawing arm should be reaching forward as much as possible while still being held by the muscles of the back. Shoulder positioning needs to be held such that the archer would barely see his drawing scapula peaking out if he stood shooting into a mirror. Practicing with a form strap will help the archer learn to twist through the body, hold with the back, and create a more compact and powerful position.

The telltale mark of holding with the hands and not with the back is the position of the drawing elbow. At the setup position the drawing elbow should be well forward of the drawing shoulder position: the drawing elbow should be forward of 90 degrees from the shoulder, making the arm an obtuse angle. If the drawing elbow is behind 90 degrees, the elbow is bent less than 90 degrees, meaning all the power is held within the arm and biceps muscle. See figure 9.3 for an example of correct drawing elbow positioning.

FIGURE 9.4

Notice the forward positioning of the draw hand as it is almost in line with the drawing arm biceps. Holding intensity is noted by the faded red circle, low in the trapezius muscle underneath the drawing scapula. The bow arm shoulder is down and forward. The bow arm triceps muscle is activated in the red circle. The final red line on the drawing shoulder indicates that the archer is reaching forward to the target and his elbow is forward of 90 degrees.

FIGURE 9.5

Here we can see the setup position from in front of the archer. Notice how the draw hand is elevated approximately as high as the nose. Pay close attention to the line of the arrow and the stabilizer of the bow indicating its direction. Now notice how the drawing elbow is almost already behind the arrow line (if one is able to imagine this three dimensional picture in his head), and that he now must draw inwards to his body. This is correct positioning.

9 SETUP POSITION

FIGURE 9.6

In the photo on the left side, notice how the arrow and stabilizer point slightly to the left. This indicates the cocked position of the bow at the setup position, which makes for easier angular drawing. If the arrow and stabilizer are already pointing straight at the target at the setup position, it is impossible to draw angularly because the body is not able to move naturally. This angling is one of the most critical elements of the setup position because angular drawing cannot be accomplished without it. The yellow line indicates the line of the arrow and shows how the archer's drawing elbow is already almost behind the line of the arrow, though he has not even started to draw the bow. This pre-alignment makes it much easier to achieve final correct alignment. The right photo shows a similar view, but from a slightly higher perspective. It is easy to see how the bow is rotated to the left of the aiming point, pivoted away from the target (the target is straight forward).

Most archers interpret angular drawing and a bent-outward wrist to mean they should have a large lateral distance, (parallel with the shooting line), between the drawing hand and the bow arm at the setup position. This is decidedly not the case – the more compact the archer can make his positioning, generally, the stronger he will be. The drawing shoulder should be held in position (remembering the pencil), with the direction of intensity as close to perpendicular with the line of the arrow as possible to create the strongest angular positioning for drawing. This position also has the drawing elbow well forward of the 90 degree angle written of earlier. If an arrow were to be placed on the shoulder blades, it would point well past the target to the right from the archer's perspective, assuming a right handed archer. The line extending forward from the arrow nocked on the string will point to the left of the target from the perspective of a right handed archer. This means the bow is cocked askew to the face of the target, even though the forward direction of the bow arm reaches toward the target. Figure 9.6 helps to understand these directions.

With the setup position now complete, the archer must have his entire mindset on angular drawing.

Review

The setup position is an important preparation for drawing, even though the archer might not distinctly stop or pause the drawing motions. When raising the bow at the target and as the archer begins to settle at the target, he must take steps through the setup position to reify his sense of direction before drawing the bow angularly.

The key elements to remember about the setup position are:

• angularly directed muscle intensity should feel like a tightening through the body

• at the setup position and at the start of drawing, the drawing elbow should be forward of a line perpendicular to the shoulder

• the bow arm reaches forward at the target such that a V is created in the top of the bow arm shoulder

• the LAN 2 is the first part to move for drawing – if the elbow is the first to move it is not possible to angularly draw the bow

• the drawing wrist should be the highest vertically elevated part of the drawing unit and should not be higher than the nose

The setup position is a continuation of most of the concepts of the set position. The head position must be perfectly maintained. Body control and posture must remain the same. All that has really changed between the set and setup positions is that now the bow has been raised to the target and the archer is ready to angularly draw the bow. There should be minimal movement between the set and setup positions because any movement that is not angular in nature is not contributing to the ultimate goal of angularly drawing the bow.

10 Angular Motion

The Oxford English Dictionary defines angular motion as "physical properties or quantities measured with reference to angles, especially those associated with rotation."

Rotation is nothing more than twisting the top off a soda bottle. Angular motion is this same twisting of the cap off the soda bottle, but more specifically, it is the physical action of the twisting: the motion one's hand follows to complete the twist.

Archery has adopted angular motion as its mantra because turning motions wind the powerful forces of the body together, allowing archers to shoot 50 pound bows without shaking. The same concept of twisting to create power and strength is found in nearly every other sport, so it is only natural to see why it is in archery as well. Golfers twist through their torsos to generate club head speed, kayakers twist through their hips and shoulders in a synchronized rotation that uses their legs to drive the boat forward, and baseball players use a 'windup' to project the power of their legs through their throwing arms. Throughout all sports, turning motions are used to hold and generate power, control, and precision.

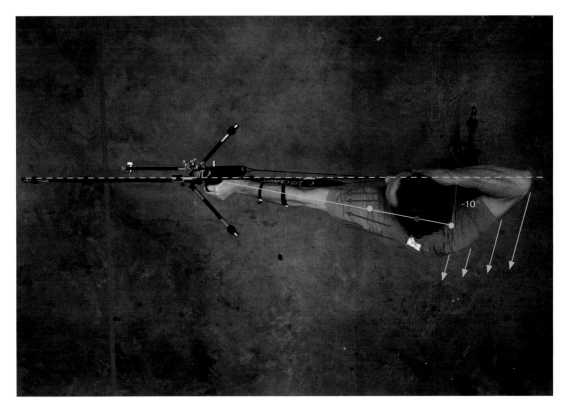

FIGURE 10.1

Here we can see proper shoulder alignment at the holding position. The shoulders make a ~10 degree angle with the line of the arrow. For expansion, the archer increases his holding sensation, exerting power along the lines of force as depicted by the red and yellow vectors. The drawing shoulder rotates around the red dot representing the spine, moving tangentially along the yellow vectors. The bow shoulder reaches toward the target with equal and opposite power along the red vectors. Ultimately this results in a net total opening of the chest.

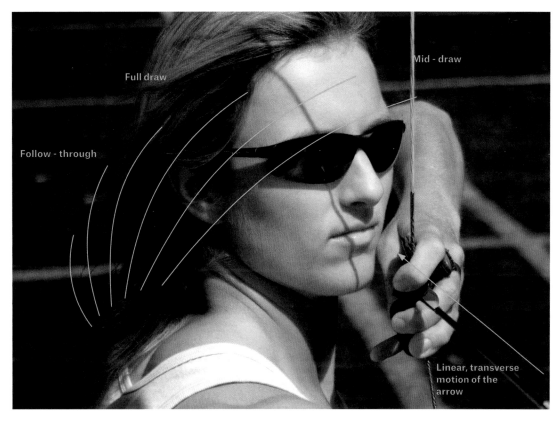

FIGURE 10.2

This diagram shows the progression of the arm as it moves through angular drawing. The archer is at mid-draw in the beginning of this photo. With rotation, small movements of the shoulder and LAN 2 produce very large movements of the drawing arm and elbow. See the curving lines connecting each of the positions. (Imagine three dimensions, the yellow lines are arcing back into the page at the level of her shoulders, not vertically toward the sky.) This is angular direction and movement. Notice how even though the shoulder is rotating around, the arrow is moving linearly towards the face. Thus, rotational motion of the shoulder unit causes linear motion of the draw hand and arrow toward the face and anchor position.

In archery, the first main concept of angular motion that must be understood is that though the shoulder, the source of the angular motion, rotates, the drawing hand moves linearly! Many archers and coaches alike fail to understand this concept by thinking the hand must move in an arc. Instead, think of a standard piston-engine in a car. The piston, the archer's arm, is connected to the crank shaft, which is the drawing arm shoulder and scapula unit of the archer. The crank shaft rotates, and because it is connected to the piston it moves the piston up and down in a straight line, even though the crank shaft is rotating! The shoulder rotates to move the arm linearly back to full draw. Remember that all the torque is being generated angularly at the shoulder – the shoulder makes the hand move linearly, and not the other way around. (In a car engine, the opposite is true. An explosion in the combustion chamber drives the piston linearly up and down, and the piston's linear energy is translated into rotational energy through the crank shaft.)

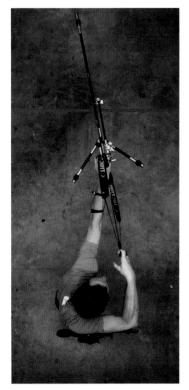  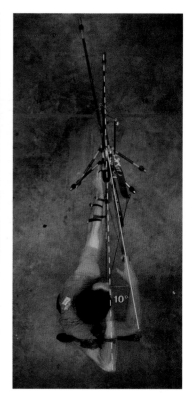

FIGURE 10.3

Here we can see an overhead view showing the archer moving from the setup position to the holding position. The bow clearly points at an angle at the setup position, rotating ~10 degrees during drawing. It is critical to maintain the bowhand thumb pressure point while the bow rotates. Notice how the alignment of the elbow remains in line with the arrow the entire time. The red arrow shows how the sight pin moves from left to right due to the rotation (see figure 8.7).

Angular rotation with tangent lines

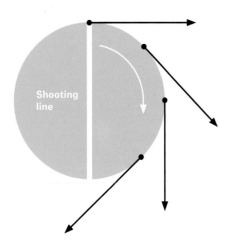

FIGURE 10.4

This picture shows angular direction as it should be understood. The white line represents an easily understood idea of angular motion – a curved line. However, the straight black lines represent what is actually going on. The straight black lines are the lines tangent to the curve at each instantaneous moment. So angular motion can be thought of as continually changing linear direction, as long as the continually changing linear directions follow the path of a curve. If we connect the black dots, notice how they form a curve, just like the white line inside the circle. This now carries a greater message: at each moment of the draw, the actual direction the archer should visualize is the straight line tangent to the curve, as this is the actual direction of the angular motion. For instance, let us assume that the black line pointing straight down represents the archer at the holding position. Expansion, then, would be in the direction of the black line. If the archer had a slightly better holding position, as perhaps can be represented by the black line angling towards the low left corner, then the direction for expansion would follow that black line. By the same corollary, the earlier black lines could represent the direction of force at the setup position, during drawing, or at the loading and anchor positions. To help with these visualizations, imagine the black dots as the drawing shoulder at various positions of the draw. The lines then help represent the instantaneous torque of the shoulder.

Counterclockwise rotation

Clockwise rotation

FIGURE 10.5

This picture explains the correct understanding of Newton's third law and how it applies to the equal and opposite reactions in archery. As has been explained, the goal of angular rotation is to move the drawing shoulder unit and LAN 2 around the body. As seen from directly above as in figure 10.1, on a right handed archer, this would be moving the LAN 2 in a clockwise direction. The archer is doing a clockwise torque. Then, at the moment of release, the fingers let go of the string and the clockwise torque of the drawing shoulder now has an equal and

opposite torque in the front half of the shot. This means that the bow arm side reacts with a counterclockwise torque. From the archer's perspective, if he is right handed, this means that his bow arm should break to the left. The two halves of the body hinge toward each other behind the archer's back centered on his spine, one side rotating clockwise and the other rotating counterclockwise. A weak or collapsed shot happens if the drawing shoulder actually rotates counterclockwise at the release.

10 ANGULAR MOTION

Should the draw hand move in an arc, this would make the elbow joint an axis of rotation, which would not aid the shoulder in its own angular motion. Linear does not only mean straight up or down, or side to side. Linear means any straight line, in any direction. Our perspective is invested in the way we see the earth and the horizon: flat. We think the shooting line is straight, and the line to the target, perpendicular to that, is straight as well. Most people would describe any straight line that does not point in these same directions as being a diagonal. This is acceptable vernacular, but remember that diagonal lines are linear too. A line that is not linear is one that curves.

The techniques to execute a shot by the teachings of this book hinge on a pivot point through the spine. The spine becomes the central reference for the archer's total angular motion – a natural halving point of the body, separating right from left, and front from back. The muscles of the back are connected to the spine, where the archer feels most closely connected with his power.

The barrel of the gun is a concept that uses the angular power of the shot to maintain a linear direction at the target. Using the spine as the main pivot point, a line is created from the drawing shoulder through the front shoulder and down the bow arm. See figure 10.1 for a picture depicting the barrel of the gun. Upon release and follow-through, the drawing arm and shoulder continue to rotate back around as depicted by the arrows in figure 10.1, or by the shapes in figure 10.2. The barrel of the gun is maintained as the shoulder rotates. The force the archer should feel is led by the rotational direction of the LAN 2. If this directional force is lost or changes direction, the barrel of the gun will break as the drawing shoulder collapses forward or the bow arm shoulder caves outwards. It is the archer's job to maintain the barrel of the gun throughout the entire shot, and especially on the release and through the follow-through.

Review

Angular motion is the whole name of the game in archery. There is nothing more important and there is nothing else any archer should concentrate on. Drawing with angular motion does not necessarily mean that the drawing hand should move in an arc, instead it is the drawing shoulder and LAN 2 that should move angularly. Angular motion should be understood and thought of as multiple connected instantaneous linear motions. This understanding will help to give better understanding of intensity and direction at the start of drawing (Chapter 11), at the loading position (Chapter 12), and during expansion (Chapter 17).

The key elements to remember about angular motion are:

• angular motion is actually multiple connected linear motions whose change of starting and ending positions form an arc

• angular motion requires an axis of rotation – for archery, this axis is the spine

• angular motion in the drawing shoulder causes linear movement of the drawing hand

• small angular motions in the drawing shoulder create large motions in the drawing elbow – the upper arm acts as a lever, increasing elbow displacement in multiples that of drawing shoulder displacement

• angular motion should never reverse direction – this is especially important at the moment of release

Angular motion is used to describe any of the major motions and positions of shooting a bow: set position (Chapter 8), drawing (Chapter 11), loading position (Chapter 12), transfer (Chapter 15), expansion (Chapter 17), release (Chapter 18), and follow-through (Chapter 20). It is the biggest and broadest reaching concept of shooting that must be fully embraced to take shooting to the next level.

The Physics of Angular Motion

By definition, angular motion needs a pivot point or axis around which to measure changes of angle. There is a difference between a physics-based definition of a pivot point and a biomechanical one. For archery, a physics definition is trumped by the biomechanical as they relate to the way the archer feels and experiences the rotational force.

Within an archer's body, it should be immediately apparent that there is more than one pivot point. The drawing shoulder rotates around at least one, and the bow arm around another. There are pivot points that move while drawing because the arc of the drawing motions becomes more tightly wound throughout the motion. Upon release, the bow shoulder and arm also react to the shot, introducing at least one more pivot point and a secondary, or tertiary, rotational system. Is it really possible for an archer to think about multiple moving pivot points while he is drawing? No. The muscles and ligaments that connect the bones are hardly consistent materials. They absorb energy, they move in all types of mathematically indescribable ways, and they generally create a system that is not what scientists would describe as "ideal." To imagine an ideal system, think of a little boy sitting on a see-saw. Push on one end and he will go up or down in direct relation to the force applied, and in a way that is easily described. Clearly the human body is not so simple as a piece of wood balanced over a fulcrum. But perhaps the most compelling part of the argument why a physics definition does

This diagram shows the concept that the circle that describes the correct motion of expansion is actually well in front of the archer, not even inside his body! Notice the clearance of the bowstring with the front shoulder and see the alignment from the drawing shoulder down through the body to the bow hand in the grip.

not help an archer is that it is easy to underestimate just how large of a circle angular motion is describing. During expansion, this book tells archers to move the LAN 2 until its arc is near parallel with the shooting line. Figure 10.4 shows what this means. However, as we start to trace the continued arc of the changing elbow positions for expansion, which is described as near parallel to the shooting line, we begin to see the circle is gigantic. The take home point is that the axis around which the elbow moves during expansion is possibly 1 or 2 meters in front of the archer! (See the previous page) Why would an archer who is attempting to control his body with the utmost precision place his focus 2 meters away? He should not, which has been explained in greater detail while examining a more biomechanical, feeling-based pivot point.

There are four sets of joints that could serve as biomechanical pivot points. The right and left shoulders, the spine, and bow arm elbow joint. These places of the body allow it's structure to hinge and bend, and are naturally the first places to look. The bow arm elbow can quickly be ruled out as it should not bend while shooting. The drawing shoulder can also be ruled out because it is the entire shoulder unit that the archer is attempting to move. The shoulder joint does hinge some while shooting, however it is not from where the primary motion comes at the moment of expansion. Arguments could be made for putting the pivot point through either the spine or the front shoulder, likely without much difference in their outcome. All the teachings in this book focus on the spine as the axis.

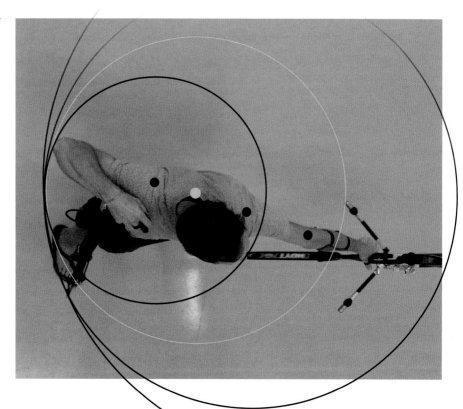

The yellow dot serves as the natural halving point of the body. The other dots throw off how the body naturally moves, making their usage as pivot less meaningful. Notice how the drawing elbow comes into final alignment with the shoulders upon release reaching a state of equilibrium where the shooting forces are balanced.

THE PHYSICS OF ANGULAR MOTION

11 Drawing

Drawing a bow is the most recognizable motion of archery.

Upon hearing the word "archery," neophytes immediately attempt some type of drawing motion, pushing one arm straight and pulling the other back by their face. By its technical description, drawing is the dynamic, angular loading of intensity within the muscles of the back, caused by turning the shoulder and scapula unit around the head, displacing the string and arrow a distance measured as the draw-length. Specifically for techniques outlined in this book, drawing starts at the setup position and lasts until the loading position. It is the largest movement an archer completes and thus one of the most important. The archer may have correctly executed all the steps prior to drawing, but without angular drawing it is impossible to achieve the angular loading, transfer, and holding necessary to shoot clean and balanced shots.

Understanding the concept of angular movement (Chapter 10), is very critical to understanding the motion and muscular control for drawing. Starting the angular holding at the set and setup positions, establishing eye focus prior to raising the bow, and providing the correct direction with the bow arm are equally important, and must be done as well. Holding a 60/40 ratio of power and intensity in the back muscles while at the setup position serves as the guiding force for the intensity of the drawing motion. See figure 11.6 for how the ratio of holding between the back muscles and the arm muscles progresses through the draw. Transferring the force the archer uses to draw the bow from the arm to the back must be smooth and recursive for consistent angular drawing, until the loading position is achieved.

FIGURE 11.1

This archer is in the middle of the drawing phase. Notice how the hand and wrist is just at the nose, the bow arm provides good direction at the target, and she leads with the LAN 2, moving away, into the picture.

Wrist bent out – Direction of LAN 2 movement   **Direction of hand movement with angular drawing**

FIGURE 11.2

The LAN 2 moves out and away from the body (toward the left side of the photo), allowing the shoulder to turn in on itself. Also notice how the thumb stretches back to keep the wrist bent out and the hand curved along the backside of the fingers. In the second photo, notice the small red line between the hand and the chin. This is the path the hand must follow to the face. The arrow describing the angular movement of the shoulder is not pointing down, imagine instead it is pointing to the right side and coming out of the page, at the reader.

Movement in the LAN 2 drives the angular drawing motion and must be the object of the archer's focus. First, the archer must hold intensity within his back at the set position, building this intensity while raising the bow at the target and coming to the setup position. Then he must use LAN 2 movement in the proper angular direction to achieve an increase of the intensity he has held and developed. The archer's job is to keep his awareness peaked on the holding intensity, making sure the holding ratio never decreases back in favor of the hands. A coach can notice a loss in scapular positioning or a lack of LAN 2 movement, but it is the archer who must ultimately remain honest with himself about his angular motion. It is the single-minded goal and focus of the archer to draw with angular motion, step inside the bow to hold with the lowest degree of effort, and control the angular expansion through the clicker. If the bow is not drawn with angular motion then it is impossible to maintain and increase the ratio of holding with the back as compared to the hands.

These esoteric discussions are important, but the actual doing is the end goal. Practice! Like most drills in archery, the archer should stand facing a mirror as though it was the target. Coming to the setup position and pausing, the draw hand should now be at its furthest lateral distance from the body. Keep in mind all the key components of the setup position and ensure these points are being maintained. Now, for the drawing motion, the hand should move in a straight line toward the face, specifically directed toward ending at the loading position (detailed in the following Chapter). This means the hand should only move inward, towards the face, as the shoulder rotates around in the drawing motion. The hand should move in a straight line because the LAN 2 is moving angularly. The arm is the rod connected to the angularly moving shoulder – rotational motion in the shoulder generates linear motion from the hand.

FIGURE 11.3

Here you can see the wrist is bent both up and out, with the elbow below the wrist. You can also see the bulging drawing scapula, moving around (toward the left side of the photo) as the archer completes the powerful drawing motion.

FIGURE 11.4

Here we see an archer just starting drawing. His drawing wrist is at a higher elevation than the elbow, as can be seen with the red lines. His butt is tucked in and under, resulting in a flat back. His forward head position gives him space to rotate around with the LAN 2 in a powerful drawing motion.

This point is one of the most misunderstood concepts of angular motion – most believe the hand should move in an arching path, out and around, to the face. If the hand does not move continually inward during the drawing motion, then the archer is losing the connection to his back and no longer will be able to load or transfer correctly. With continual angular motion from the LAN 2 and shoulder unit, the hand must only move inwards. If the archer or coach sees the hand either move outwards or remain at the same lateral distance from the face (not move inwards toward the face), then angular drawing has changed to linear drawing and the shot is lost. The archer must spend many hours in front of the mirror watching himself complete this motion to ensure physical understanding and create muscle memory. Angular drawing means rotational motion from the shoulder, as in figure 11.2.

There is a similar concept for the vertical aspect of drawing. At the setup position the drawing hand should be at its highest vertical position, just as it is at its most outward lateral position. As discussed in "Setup Position," Chapter 9, this highest vertical position should be no higher than the nose. From its vertical peak, the hand should move in a straight line to the loading position. The loading position – the archer's goal of drawing – is just below the chin, and well below the height of the hand at setup position, so the hand should never move without a vertical component and should never go upwards. Bringing the hand uniformly down while drawing creates the low position of the drawing scapula that is the biomechanically strongest to hold the force of the bow.

It is best to talk about drawing a bow through alignment and direction rather than muscle control, however it should be noted that if done correctly, the focal point of the muscle intensity will be located in the low trapezius muscle underneath the drawing scapula. Nearly all of the muscles supporting and controlling the shoulder will be used to hold the bow, however the greatest focus should be on the low trapezius muscle. This is because LAN 2 movement, out the back of the body, is generated most by the low trapezius muscle. Since LAN 2 movement is the object for drawing the bow, the byproduct is increased muscle intensity of the muscles controlling LAN 2 movement.

FIGURE 11.5

Here we see an archer almost at the loading position, near the end of the draw. Notice how flat his drawing arm looks in comparison with the arrow. Especially notice the position of the elbow and how it is neither higher nor lower than the line of the arrow, as represented by the yellow line. They are nearly parallel. This is correct positioning as it puts the force of the archer directly in alignment with what will become the forward force of the arrow.

Ratio of holding with the back muscles/hands

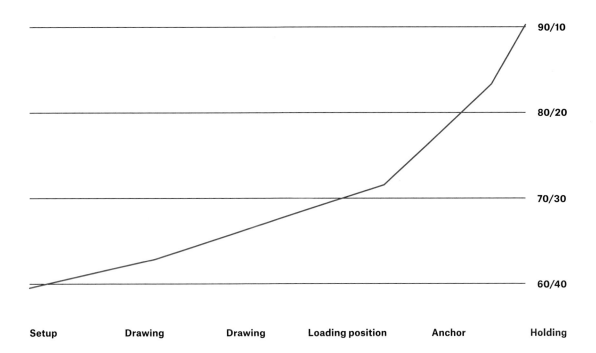

FIGURE 11.6

This chart shows how the ratio of the strength in the muscles of the back and in the muscles of the arm and hand changes during drawing, through the loading position, and to holding. For instance, the bow may only require 30 pounds of force to be held at the setup position. The 60/40 ratio means that approximately 18 pounds is being held with the back muscles and 12 is held with the hand. Because drawing the bow farther increases the force required ('drawing force'), the force may be 50 pounds at full-draw. A 90/10 ratio means that 45 pounds is being held with the back muscles and only 5 pounds is held with the fingers. The graph starts to curve because as the archer draws closer to the loading and holding positions, the faster the ratio must change. The more angularly the archer draws and gets closer to having his elbow completely behind the arrow, the more he can, and should, use his back muscles to draw and hold the bow.

The bow arm has a simple and straightforward task during drawing: maintain pressure and direction through the pressure point of the hand on the grip while remaining pointed at the target. It is common for the bow arm shoulder to rise up as the weight of the bow increases. This must be resisted by keeping all the elements of a correct bow arm. For reference, refer back to Chapter 7, "Bow Arm." The worst that can happen to the bow arm during drawing is for the elbow to lose its twist. Should this happen it is almost guaranteed the archer will hit his arm, a very painful experience that can quickly ruin archers. By keeping a tight triceps muscle and maintaining a strong pressure point in the grip, unwanted bow arm rotation can be prevented. Another common ailment would be the bow arm shoulder rolling in towards the string during drawing, especially just before the loading position. An archer may be over-bowed when this happens, and needs to go down to a lower draw weight.

FIGURE 11.7

The following three sets of pictures are among the most important in the book. All three archers feel muscle intensity in their backs while drawing the bow, although they use drastically different techniques. The top example is a near-perfect example that should be used as a guideline. From the setup position, the draw is completely towards the body, as indicated by the long black line. The black line in the top series of photos barely moves downwards from its elevation at the setup position. The second photo of the top example shows the archer at the loading position, and the third photo at the anchor/holding position. There is a very small movement up to the chin between the loading position and the anchor/holding position as indicated by the very short black line. A key thing to notice is that the black line continues to move closer to the body even while anchoring, indicating that rotation never stops taking place. The red line then indicates a horizontal, parallel with the shooting line, transfer. The yellow line then shows an indicated perfect release motion, along with the slightly curved actual elbow release motion. Notice how in the top example the double yellow line appears almost as one line. Now we contrast this with the middle example, which shows the drawing elbow actually moving away from the body while drawing! This is not any angular movement at all. Then the elbow moves almost vertically up to the anchor position, with considerably more vertical movement than in the first example. Upon release, the elbow falls away from the desired movement along the line of the arm. The bottom example shows some angular motion, however it has too much vertical motion in both the drawing and the anchoring segments. Also, the transfer motion indicated by the red line is more up than it is around, indicating no additional angular motion. The release follows the desired path.

FIGURE 11.8

Two archers photographed at setup position (1), the loading position (2), and the holding position (3). Here we can clearly see any vertical changes in drawing elbow and drawing hand elevation. The red line represents the path of the point of the drawing elbow. In the top set of photos, notice how small the change in elbow elevation is. Contrast this with the bottom set of photos, showing a very large movement. Neither archer raises their drawing elbow or hand before achieving loading position. The elbow change should be somewhere in between the two set of photos. It should be no smaller than the example on the top and no larger than the bottom example. For most archers it is easier to maintain connection with the back muscles if they have movement more similar to the top example.

11 DRAWING

The drawing must be smooth and fluid. Chapter 14, "Rhythm," and Chapter 27," Putting It All Together," continue the discussion on fluidity. At no time should there be any jerking sensations, loss of body control, leaning, head position changes, or staccato, choppy motions. The power of drawing comes from deep in the core and abdomen. Connection must be maintained or the shot will be lost. An archer needs grace to calmly reach the loading position, having already contained the holding balance of the bow between the two halves of the body.

Drawing is the fastest element out of drawing, loading, anchor, and transfer. The entire motion lasts barely more than half a second, and never more than a full second. Should the archer gingerly and carefully draw the bow, all fluidity is lost and the rhythm of the shot is thrown off. On the other extreme, the bow should not be jerked back as quickly as possible. There is a balance in between where power and grace are both maintained and the greatest degree of control can be utilized. The bow should be drawn with the latter. The key to maintaining this fluidity is transitioning smoothly and correctly through the different technique elements, slowing down and speeding up the motion of raising the bow, drawing, anchoring, and shooting. For instance, when the archer raises his bow at the target and begins to settle down to the setup position, he is slowing down and stopping his vertical motion and transitioning to the flatter angular drawing motion. In some ways you could say he is pausing, preparing for another set of motions, and so he is. This is similar to a golfer pausing his upswing, coiling his body, and transitioning into his downswing. Archers must have this same pause, this same transition, as they start to draw the bow, and again as they transition from drawing, through the loading position, to the anchor. Smooth speed transitions, both faster and slower, are the only way an archer can maintain control while shooting.

Review

Using the concepts learned in Chapter 10, "Angular Motion," and in Chapter 9, "Setup Position," drawing begins immediately after reaching the setup position and lasts until the loading position (Chapter 12).

Drawing is the transition from the setup position to the loading position. The transition must occur smoothly and seamlessly, without jerking or choppiness. The speedup and slowdown of motion needed to accomplish a smooth draw are described in Chapter 14, "Rhythm." In its entirety, drawing must be of angular direction.

The key elements to remember about drawing are:

• while the drawing shoulder moves angularly around the body, the drawing hand moves linearly toward the face

• at the setup position, the drawing hand is at its highest vertical position and its farthest outward position horizontally – during drawing, the drawing hand only moves inward and downward toward the loading position (see figure 11.7)

• it is especially important to maintain the hooking position and wrist position established at the set position (note: this is difficult to do)

• the drawing motion should be led by the LAN 2

• the muscular intensity of drawing should grow in ratio of the back muscles to the arm muscles (see figure 11.6)

• drawing must be very smooth and fluid

As is outlined in the following Chapter, "Loading Position," the archer must feel 90 percent ready to shoot the arrow at the loading position. Drawing culminates at the loading position, and so drawing slows down for the archer to prepare himself. This amount of holding and readiness is outlined in Chapter 14, "Rhythm." Correct angular drawing continues through the loading position and anchor positions, and into transfer and expansion. The angular motion never stops through any of these movements or positions.

12 Loading Position

———

The loading position occurs at the end of the drawing phase when the archer reaches "the wall" with his angular rotation.

The archer has reached the wall when, during angular drawing, the shoulder has rotated to almost its maximum amount of rotation, and he senses he cannot rotate much further. More movement will come in the following steps of transfer and expansion, but these movements are very small. Think about sitting down while leaning against a wall, but without a chair below. There is a sensation, when the thighs are almost parallel with the ground, of sitting in a chair. It is possible to squat all the way down and rest on the feet, however this does not give a sitting sensation. The loading position is a similar position: it is possible to rotate just a little bit farther, but doing so would take the body out of balance.

This angular storing of the drawing energy within the core of the body is a key step in creating the control necessary for fluid, balanced, and beautiful shooting. More specifically, loading is a preparation step, much like the set or setup positions. It is a preparatory step because it is not the actual act of drawing a bow or shooting the arrow – loading is not an active motion; one should think of it as a position. It is not possible to load to the loading position, one draws to the loading position, where the angular torque is created. The distinction is important because it

Loading position too low, 4 - 5 inches below the jaw

Correct loading position, slightly more than one inch

FIGURE 12.1

It is easy to see the differences in the loading positions shown in these two photographs. In both photos the archer is achieving the loading position, but in the second photo there is an easier transition to the anchor position. In the first photo his drawing unit (arm, hand, and shoulder) is in an unnaturally low position where greater skill, control, and time is needed to achieve anchor position without disconnecting from his back muscles. Contrast this with the second photo where we see an archer who is compact and tight against

his body, his drawing hand is already tight against his neck, and the string is already pushing into his face where it will rest at the anchor position. It is important to note that tightness of the hand or string against the neck or face is not what characterizes a good loading position, as what is most important is the amount of drawing shoulder rotation that is held and the location of the muscle intensity to hold this position. Achieving a loading position that is tight into the body will only make the position stronger.

FIGURE 12.2

Here we can see the archer at the loading position just prior to anchor. Notice how there is a substantial gap between the right and left scapulae as this archer has executed loading correctly. He is rotating his shoulder and is not pinching or squeezing the low trapezius and rhomboid muscles of the drawing side toward the spine. Drawing and loading are angular motions, which is described and noticed as a winging motion of the scapula (in this picture, it is seen as the LAN 2 moving out of the page), instead of pinching toward the spine. The highlighted area shows the main position of the holding power. Be aware that all of the muscles of the back and shoulder are used to some degree, just at the highest concentrations in the highlighted area.

indicates drawing must be complete, meaning one has reached the loading position. Now, with the full feeling of the drawing intensity, the archer can continue the angular progression of force by taking the anchor position and following with transfer. Too often archers attempt to rush through the loading position without fully controlling the holding intensity of the body and end up losing the fluidity of the shot that comes from drawing the bow.

Loading position   **Anchor position**

FIGURE 12.3

Pay close attention to the position of the drawing elbow elevation. A straight line was measured from the tip of the elbow in the loading picture over to the anchor picture. The bottom of the yellow line in the anchor picture is the position of the elbow at loading and the top is the position at anchor. Notice there is zero change in the posture, head positioning, shoulder alignment, and shoulder elevation. There must be minimal movement between loading and anchor to ensure the highest levels of control.

The loading position is achieved when the drawing hand is just underneath the chin and the drawing scapula has sufficiently stored the angular intensity of drawing within the powerful muscles of the back. The drawing hand should be no more than two inches below the jaw at the loading position. See figure 12.1 for examples of loading too low and loading correctly. If one loads too low it is not possible to smoothly transition to the anchor position. Though not always the case, the string should touch the chin at the same position as it does for the anchor position. The string should not slide transversely along the jaw between the loading position and the anchor position. Often the drawing hand thumb is securely pressed against the sternomastoid muscle. This particular reference point, drawing until the thumb is pressed tightly into the neck, is a very good way to draw consistently to the same loading position. However, it can also cause an archer to bend his drawing hand wrist the wrong way. Remember, the wrist and thumb must stay in exactly the same position as during hooking, so that drawing until the thumb presses into the neck is an effect of achieving the correct loading position not a cause. Keeping the drawing hand still must be automatic: loading can only be felt within the muscles of the back and core. This is where an archer must direct his focus. If the archer tries to think about drawing until the string touches his face or his thumb presses tightly into his neck, it will be impossible for him to hold with the correct power and direction within his back muscles because his focus was on his face.

The loading position is known as a position because very little to no motion takes place. A very small external angular motion is sometimes seen, however the majority of the action takes place under the skin. Visible movement of the scapula is limited to a slight protruding or winging of the scapula with equally minimal lateral movement of the tip of the scapula toward the spine. There is potentially a small downward, toward the ground, movement of the scapula upon reaching the loading position. None of these motions should be more than one centimeter in any direction.

FIGURE 12.4

Here is another example of a good loading position. The draw hand thumb is tight against the neck, the string is tight against the chin, and there is only about a one inch gap between the top of the drawing hand and the chin. Also, notice how the chin is lifted, almost parallel with the ground, allowing extra space under the jaw for a comfortable and easy anchor position.

12 LOADING POSITION

Instead of external motion, one should think of loading as an internal storing of drawing intensity. Thought about in terms of percentages, one begins to draw the bow 40 percent with the arms, and 60 percent with the muscles of the back. With an angular drawing technique as described in Chapter 11, "Drawing," the ratio grows in favor of the back muscles. At the loading position, this ratio should be approximately 80 percent back, and 20 percent hands and arm. As per techniques described in Chapter 15, "Transfer," and Chapter 16, "Holding," the holding power should already be transferred to the back at the loading position. The loading position is nearly full holding with the back. Loading prepares the body for the final transfer to the complete holding position. It is not possible to transfer from 0 holding to 90 percent holding during the transfer phase, although many archers seem to believe this to be so. The entire point of angular drawing is to transition as much of the holding force as possible into the back muscles without compromising a secure hook on the string. Refer back to figure 11.6 which showed this concept in a graph. Remember that the closer one gets to the loading position, the greater the capacity he has to hold the force of the bow with his back muscles. Early in the draw, the ratio does not change as quickly as it does in the final inches of the draw.

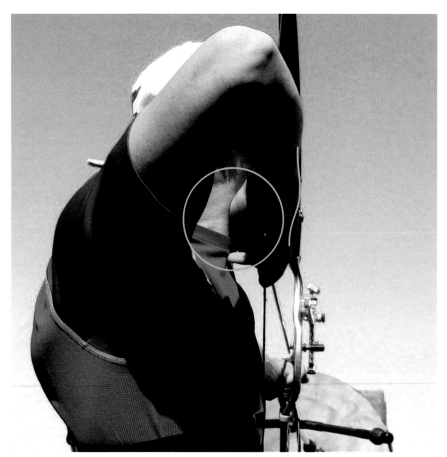

FIGURE 12.5

Here we can see the drawing hand thumb pressed tightly into the sternomastoid muscle of the neck. The pinky is also touching the neck. Both of these reference points can be used when checking for a full and complete loading position. Notice how the drawing elbow is already fully behind the arrow. Most importantly, notice how the drawing hand wrist is still bent outwards.

Setup position

Loading position

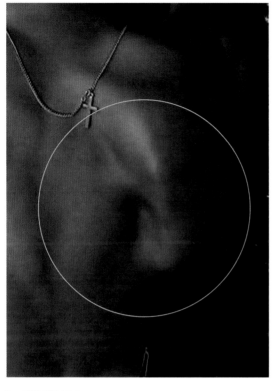 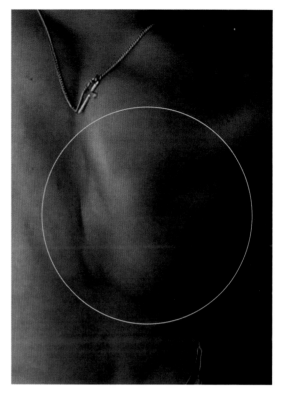

FIGURE 12.6

Notice how the scapula position changes during drawing. At the loading position, we can see the lower trapezius muscle holding down the edge of the scapula.

Also, we can see that the shoulder position has moved three dimensionally, more out of the page.

Nearly the same amount of control and conscious awareness of holding that the archer uses at full draw needs to be used at the loading position. Because of this, there needs to be a slight slowing of the drawing motion at the loading position. Here the archer takes about a half-second to control the energy stored within his back, and then he can begin raising upward to the anchor position while maintaining scapular positioning in his back. There should be a smooth slowing of the drawing motion just before achieving the full loading position, a brief moment of visible stillness, and then motion begins again as the archer begins moving the hand up to the anchor position. Too many archers skip this slowing because they are thinking they need to hurry up and reach anchor so they can transfer and begin trying to shoot the shot. The archer needs a moment to control, balance, and hold the angular drawing intensities before going on with the shot. Much as the archer needs to take a moment to control the torque of transfer before going on to expansion (refer to Chapter 15, "Transfer," for continuing details), the archer must also take a brief moment to control the drawing and loading intensities before anchoring.

It is important to realize the act of loading is not a pinching, squeezing, or contracting of the muscles of the back. The loading position is a position of power, not of muscle contraction induced shaking. To exert great power one should not think of the muscles contracting; instead think of containing and controlling the power and energy in the direction you wish it to go. For archery, one should think of the angular storing of the drawing intensity within the core of the body. At the loading position the archer should feel the balanced power of the bow, then and only then can he move on to anchor, and to the subsequent steps of the shot.

While moving upward to the anchor position, it is very critical the holding balance that was achieved at the loading position is not lost even the tiniest amount. If the archer loses some of this control it is generally seen as the scapula moving upward and away from the spine as the draw hand moves up to the anchor position. There should never be any negative movement of the LAN 2 and scapula throughout the entire drawing, loading, anchoring, transfer, expansion, execution, and follow-through phases. Negative movement is described as the LAN 2 or scapula reversing direction and moving back along the path from where they just came. Any negative movement means the archer has lost the connection and balance of the shot and will no longer be able to execute a clean and beautiful shot.

It is not trite to remind archers that consistency is what is ultimately important here. More specifically, consistency of the loading position is so critical, because it means that one has executed drawing correctly and is 90 percent ready to shoot the arrow. With 90 percent of the shot ready, it makes it that much easier to focus on the remaining 10 percent. Every time the archer draws his bow, he must feel the full feeling that is associated with hitting the wall at the loading position. If he is not very consistent with his intensity, angular motion, or feeling, he will have vastly different lengths to expand through the clicker, creating far greater inconsistencies. As has been mentioned earlier, the loading position is the final readying for shooting. This is why the loading position must be as consistent as possible.

Review

The loading position could be described as the position where the safety is switched off in the process of shooting. It is the dividing position between preparing to shoot the arrow, and actually completing the process of shooting. Should the clicker go off prior to completing the loading position, the archer should not feel compelled to shoot the arrow. Though the archer is 90 percent ready to shoot the arrow, prior to reaching the loading position and transitioning to the anchor position, the archer is not in the shooting phase and feels no urge to release. The loading phase is characterized by a slowing of the drawing motions, and a sensation of holding as is described at the full draw holding position in Chapter 16. The only difference in sensation between the loading position and the holding position is that the anchor occurs between them. The sensation in the back muscles must be nearly the same.

The key elements to remember about the loading position are:

• the thumb should push into the sternomastoid muscle at the loading position – this is also the same position the thumb will occupy at the anchor position

• the distance below the chin is different on all archers, though proper loading and efficient movement is required for everyone

• the string should touch the chin at the same position it does at the anchor position

• there should be minimal elbow movement between the loading and anchor positions

• the force and direction of the loading position should be that of the drawing motion while reaching the loading position – there should be no physical difference between the completion of the draw and reaching the loading position

The loading position is also the culmination of the drawing phase (Chapter 11). It connects the archer with the anchor position, leaves him 90 percent ready to shoot the arrow and only requiring minimal transfer (Chapter 15), and provides the basis of intensity and directional control for expansion (Chapter 17). Reaching a correct loading position means the hooking position and wrist position has not changed from Chapter 4. This can be especially difficult to isolate the muscles in such a fashion.

Practicing Without a Coach

The task of the archer without a coach is doubly difficult compared to his opponents. A coach is a mentor, teacher, friend, and training partner. However, it is a close relationship an archer and coach must maintain, with both of their minds remaining in harmony about the required skill and expectation of dreams. A skillful coach and a lazy archer will not produce a team that is capable of a great victory. Likewise, a determined and hardworking archer with a coach that leads him down the wrong paths will find all his efforts to be wasted. For this reason all archer/coach relationships should be approached with great care.

Many archers are not blessed with the geographic location where they can have easy access to a coach who matches their expectation from archery. Despite this difficulty, modern day technology has made it easier than ever to practice without a coach.

Most modern digital cameras record video on top of their normal picture taking abilities, allowing all archers to easily capture footage of their practices. Long term, coaching is the ability to recognize small changes in technique, something that is now possible by examining nightly videos of a training session. Each individual arrow might feel incredibly important to the beginner archer, but after he has a few years under his belt, the anxiety fades into the background and the mature archer only cares about his technique day to day, or week to week. For some, practicing without a coach is the only way they are able to find success. Two alpha personalities may often butt heads and create enough stress to negate any potential benefits in training with a coach.

At the end of the day, an archer needs to maintain his calm and composure. Practicing without a coach can sometimes be just the calm that is needed.

Video feedback is especially important when training without a coach. With a simple tripod, video camera, and monitor, consistent historicizing is possible, allowing changes to be tracked and catalogued.

PRACTICING WITHOUT A COACH

13 Anchor Position

The joining and securing of the drawing hand to the jaw, chin, and neck is known as achieving anchor position. The anchor position connects the archer to the bow and serves as the fixed rear sight.

Though the word anchor, having connotations of stopping or holding, does not have explicitly similar meanings in archery, it is accepted vernacular and will continue to be used throughout this book. As the anchor position serves as the rear sight and thus plays a role in aiming, it is a position of extreme precision as any inconsistencies from shot to shot will result in large deviations on the target. There are many details to the anchor position, which this chapter will address in a straightforward manner.

The first and most important element of the anchor position is the location of the metacarpophalangeal joint of the drawing hand top finger. At the corner of the jaw, there is a pocket between the edge of the jawbone and the musculature of the neck. It is within this pocket that the joint must be wedged to achieve an effective anchor position. See figure 13.1 for an example showing this pocket and positioning. Figure 13.4 explicitly shows the contact area on the draw hand and details the positioning of the distal joint.

Many archers fail to fully position the distal joint inside this pocket and thus tend to have anchors that slide up their face. If the joint only sits underneath the jawbone and not within the pocket, the archer will revert to an anchor that slides up his face in pressure situations, or one that is not as connected and secure. Instead of using the knuckle of the distal joint many archers will instead use the fleshy area of the hand between the thumb and top finger, commonly known as the web of the hand. By using this type of an anchor, archers will push upwards to create a solid feeling – however, due to the flexible nature of the web of the hand, this will create the upwards sliding anchor that was previously mentioned. It is of utmost importance the distal joint is fully set within the pocket between the jawbone and neck muscles to create a solid and consistent anchor position.

FIGURE 13.1

These photos show the position where the top finger rear knuckle (metacarpophalangeal joint) should tuck in underneath the jawbone to give the archer the most solid anchor possible. It is very important the knuckle fits entirely inside the pocket and does not begin to slide up the jaw and the side of the face. Though these photos show the archers before and after shooting their arrow, it provides a clear picture of the archer's jawlines, and thus the pocket where the distal joint must sit.

Center anchor **Incorrect: Too far to the side** **Correct side anchor**

  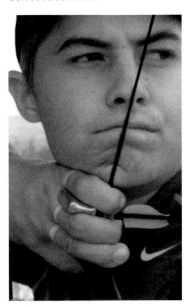

FIGURE 13.2

Notice how the center anchor tends to make the archer tilt his head position to the side to achieve the correct string alignment – this is incorrect. In the middle photo, see how the string sits to the side of the nose and is well back on the side of the chin so much that it pushes the lips up strangely to the side. Upon release, the string will drag on the chin and cause inconsistent arrow flight that cannot be adjusted by mere fine-tuning. In the last photo on the right, notice how the string sits just a little to the side of center, but is still on the front of the chin. It is not on the side of the jaw as seen in the previous photo. The string sits comfortably in the center of the nose and the head is relaxed. As a quick side note, look at the differences in the amount of hooking between the first photo and the last photo. In the last photo the top finger is hooked deeper than in the first photo. This deeper hook is a stronger position.

The second element of the anchor position is the string location on the chin and nose. Because aiming depends on the string being aligned with the upright bow at full draw, head position and anchor position are critical for proper string alignment at anchoring. Along with the amount of head rotation and tilt, the position of the string on the chin and nose serve as the critical determiners for string alignment. A side anchor position, slightly biased to the drawing side, gives the archer better clearance under the jaw for anchoring, and provides a more biomechanically advantaged position. Be careful not to go too far to the side, as there can be considerable string drag on the chin upon release. See figure 13.2 for examples of a center anchor, correct side anchor, and one that is too far to the side. High speed video analysis has shown flight inconsistencies of the arrow as it is goes through the bow if the anchor is too far to the side; for this reason it is suggested to be conservative with the side anchor. Too far, and a side anchor will cause the string to drag on the chin upon release, skewing its lateral direction. To avoid similar string clearance issues with the nose upon release, keep the string in the exact center of the nose. Doing so also provides the most consistent reference point for repeatability.

Archers commonly make facial contortions while anchoring or positioning the string on their chin. While this is a minor point compared to others mentioned here, it is important for the archer to keep his face as still and relaxed as possible while drawing, and shooting. Even small tendencies, like pursing one's lips to touch the string or tightening up the muscles of the chin while anchoring, can start a chain reaction of tension that destroys the shot. This is just another example of control that is critical for peak performance and for an archer to stay within the zone.

FIGURE 13.3

The top picture shows an incorrect anchor position that uses only the front of the top finger and leaves a substantial gap between the thumb and neck. The bottom picture shows the correct anchor position – full contact can be seen all the way throughout the hand and jaw. Within reason, the tighter the anchor, the better connected the archer will be with the muscles in the back.

FIGURE 13.4

The important highlighted contact area is where the most pressure should be felt while maintaining the anchor position. Keep the thumb stretched down and back to keep the hand in the best biomechanical position to release the string. Notice the thumb bent down and back, but still straight. Also see how the pinky is stretched back and out, but is not overly curled.

Thumb positioning is the second most misunderstood point of anchoring – second only to tucking the top knuckle into the pocket of the jaw. There are only two positions the thumb can occupy, either in front or behind the sternomastoid, the muscle running from the ear down to the throat, the muscle that sticks out when the head is turned to the side. Some archers can find an anchor with the thumb behind the sternomastoid, something on the order of around thirty percent, as the length of the jaw is short compared to the size of their hands. Only archers with very large hands and very small heads/necks should ever consider an anchor behind the jaw. For almost all archers, the correct thumb position is securely tucked into the front of the sternomastoid, at a downward angle resting against the wind-pipe. What most people do incorrectly is they lose the stretching back and down of the thumb they established when they secured their hooking position. Many people even hold the thumb against the tab in an effort to hold it in place. Others use the thumb as some type of ledge. All of these thumb positions are incorrect as they cause a higher degree of intensity and activation of the muscles in the forearm, taking away connection from the muscles in the back. By cocking the wrist outwards and the keeping thumb stretched back such that the skin in the web of the hand between the thumb and forefinger is close to taut, this allows the fingers to maintain their hook on the string while providing the most relaxed position for the forearm muscles. Because the forearm is relaxed, the archer will be less likely to try and squeeze through the clicker with either the fingers or the muscles of the arm.

Another slight clarification on the thumb position: the thumb should not have a sharp bend at the last joint that gives the thumb anything close to a 90 degree angle. While it does not have to be completely straight, it is important the thumb is nearly straight and in a relaxed position. This means the fingernail on the thumb should rest against the skin of the neck down by the Adam's apple. It is easy to feel by bending the thumb that the muscles of the hand and forearm tense.

To control the pitch of the hand at anchor position, the tip of the pinky finger must rest against the neck. Like the thumb, the pinky should not be bent so much as to add tension to the hand and cause disconnected releases. The draw hand should not be completely vertical, but it does need to be twisted in enough so the pinky can comfortably touch the neck.

Many archers are surprised with how tight or full the anchor position must feel. Some even describe the correct feeling as slightly choking. It is better for the anchor to be tighter into the neck and jaw than not, so this is not entirely a bad way to think about it. If viewed from above, there should be zero gaps anywhere. See figure 13.3 for examples of gaps and no gaps.

FIGURE 13.5

In the highlighted area, notice how the skin of the archer's neck is pulled by the drawing hand thumb and top finger joint. This archer also has a very snug anchor as seen by the lines on his face from the tightly pressed string. These are key points to a strong, connected, and consistent anchor position. The yellow line indicates an acceptable amount of inward rotation of the hand. The hand is not completely vertical, but the third finger is securely on the string.

FIGURE 13.6

The picture on the top shows an archer that has created a gap between his metacarpophalangeal joint and the rear of his jawbone. Notice how his hand actually slopes down toward his wrist. Holding this position requires considerable forearm strength from the archer. Contrast this with the picture on the bottom, showing a correct position of the metacarpophalangeal joint tucked under the jawbone. The line of the hand points upwards to the wrist.

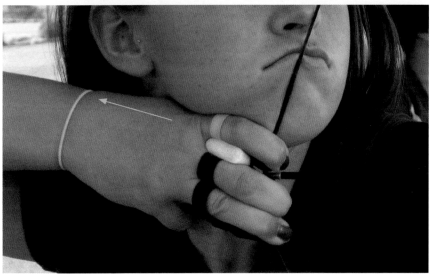

The actual pressure on the draw hand is also much farther back on the hand than most would expect. Many archers attempt to use the top finger as the main source of contact with the jaw, however this is inefficient because it does not focus on achieving the full anchor through the entire hand. The main source of contact starts at the metacarpophalangeal joint that is tucked under the jawbone into the aforementioned pocket and extends back through the hand to the first joint of the thumb. See figure 13.4 for a highlighted picture. Due to strongly slanted jawlines, some archers cannot achieve contact completely through the hand and must use more of the fingers. While not incorrect, jaw contact throughout the entire hand makes for a more powerful connection. The fingers' job is to keep their hook and allow the string to release when the moment comes. It is the job of the hand to provide the anchor position.

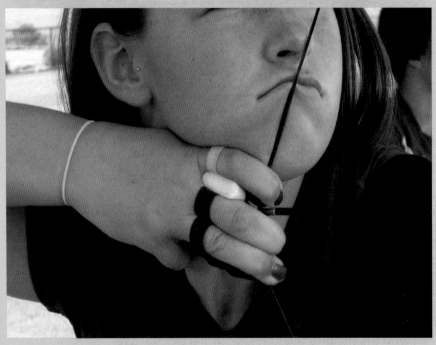

FIGURE 13.7

Notice on the top photo how the metacarpophalangeal joint is not snugged under the jawbone and is actually up the side of the cheek. Also notice how the middle finger joint pops out of the hand in the top photo, whereas it is flat in the bottom photo. The bottom photo is the correct position.

Review

The goal of the anchor position is to connect the string, arrow, and drawing hand to the core of the body and the powerful and controlling back muscles. Essentially, the more solid contact that can be achieved, the better. For this reason, it is advised to use a finger tab without a shelf, or a very small one that is not used as the main source of contact. The more of the hand and fingers than can make solid contact with the jawbone and neck, the stronger the connection will be. As the archer does not want the anchor position to move or slide during expansion (Chapter 17), there should not be a worry of creating too solid an anchor and interfering with expansion. Expansion should be felt as a turning through the body, not a sliding or changing of anchor position on the face.

The key elements to remember about the anchor position are:

• the string should sit on the corner of the chin – not in the middle, and not on the jaw

• the string should rest exactly in the center of the nose, making gentle contact

• the hooking position earlier established must remain exactly the same while coming to the anchor position

• the top finger metacarpophalangeal joint should tuck in under the pocket at the back of the jawbone

• the thumb should either fit snugly behind the sternomastoid or just in front of it, wedged between it and the windpipe

• the draw hand should be rotated near vertical so the third finger rests comfortably on the string

• the tighter the anchor the better

The anchor position is affected directly by changes in head positioning (Chapter 6). Slight changes in hooking (Chapter 4), will also negatively affect the anchor position. As the thumb position remains the same between the loading position (Chapter 12), and the anchor position, the archer only needs to ensure that thumb position does not change between these back-to-back steps. Changes in anchor positioning can also affect how an archer feels or experiences expansion (Chapter 17), and release (Chapter 18).

14 Rhythm

Rhythm,
or the systematic
arrangement of the
steps of drawing
according to the
duration and fluidity
of the movements,
is the foundation for
drawing a recurve
bow with control
and ease.

Loading position

FIGURE 14.1

This photo shows the archer at the loading position holding with his back muscles, ready for a smooth transition to anchor. Notice how the string already makes contact with the face exactly at the same place it does at anchor position. No sliding of the string forward or back occurs between these two steps.

Anchor position

FIGURE 14.2

This picture shows the same archer a few frames later when he's reached anchor. Notice how tight the hand and string are to the jaw and face. Full contact through the hand and jaw will connect the archer with his back muscles.

The rhythm of the draw can be divided into three distinct phases and corresponding keywords: loading, anchor, and transfer. When rhythm is finally learned and integrated into shooting there is an extreme sense of fluidity, and the step-step-step distinctions are replaced by smooth transitions. The changes from phase to phase will be invisible to outside observers though the archer will still feel them – the blending must be that refined. Rhythm helps eliminate hesitation and creates more consistent timing.

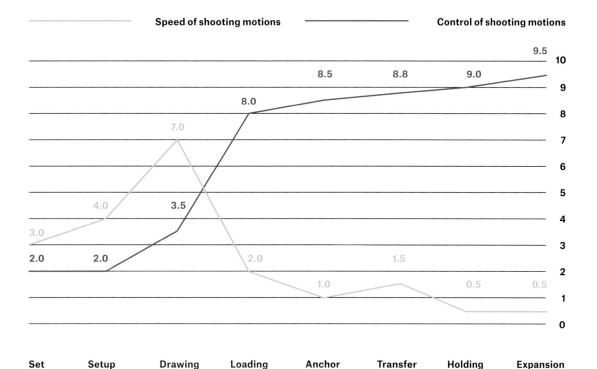

FIGURE 14.3

This graph shows the speed of drawing the bow so as to create a smooth and fluid-looking shot. Notice how midway through drawing is shown to be the fastest and most dynamic part of the shot. Clearly, this is where the archer moves the most. However, also notice that the archer never stops the drawing motions, he only slows down or slightly changes the intensity of his angular motion. Take special care to notice how the drawing motion slows as the archer approaches the loading position. It is at the loading position that the archer must begin to control the bow as if he were ready to shoot the arrow. See how similar the speed of drawing at the loading position is compared to transfer, or even expansion. As the archer slows, his control must go up inversely, as shown by the yellow line. Already at the loading position, the archer must have nearly the same control as he does when he is expanding through the clicker. Remember, the archer might only move a couple centimeters between the loading position and the expansion position, just before the clicker goes off. Prior to that, he moves nearly 20 times as much.

The result of correct rhythm is precise back muscle intensity control. These attributes are caused by the three-part draw. The first two parts of the rhythm, loading and anchor, can be thought of as preparations for shooting, not as an actual act of shooting. By completing the third phase, transfer, one is ready to expand and shoot. If the archer only complete the first two steps, the thought of the string releasing is non-existent. Distinguishing the steps of the three part draw is important because if the clicker goes off during the loading or anchor phase, the archer knows he is not yet prepared for the string to release, and thus will not do so. By comparison, with a continuous draw there is no sense of preparation while anchoring, and so the clicker could go off before the archer is ready and he will not have the control to let the bow down. Using rhythm to load, anchor, and transfer will give the archer the control that is needed in high-pressure match-play situations.

It is easiest to come to the loading, anchor, and transfer positions by counting numbers. Loading is one, anchor is two, and transfer is three. While drawing, the archer should count to himself: "oooonnneee, two, ... threeeeee." Coming to the loading position, extra time should be taken to balance out and control the drawing intensity and maintain the connection with the back muscles.

This is the reason for the drawn out "oooonnnneeee". Remember, at the loading position, an archer should feel like he is almost ready to shoot the arrow. Anchor, "two," takes a moment, but is not fast or staccato. Two flows smoothly from the loading position and should perhaps be more characterized by its softness of sound and motion, or how similarly it feels to the loading position. Again, another blending occurs as one transitions from the anchor position into the controlled turning of transfer. Like the loading position, extra time and control needs to be taken during transfer to ensure the maximum connectedness and precision. Ultimately, everything must be blended together. Intensity must flow dynamically such that one barely notices three steps. Each part must be a greater element in the total rhythm, in the total dance of shooting.

It is often difficult to stress to archers the amount of fluidity necessary for rhythm to appear controlled and beautiful. Even many advanced archers competing at world championships appear choppy or staccato with their movements. Invariably, these archers do not win the championships. To correctly achieve rhythm, the archer must master the grace of a ballerina and the sense of timing of a concert pianist. Each transition between the steps of drawing a bow must have the finesse and flowing lines of a painter's brush stroke. Drawing the bow should look more like dancing than it should the repetition of step-by-step motions. There is a considerable amount of neuromuscular control the body must learn – usually the best teacher is simply time. Fixing rhythm is not something that can be done in an afternoon like changing string alignment or anchor positioning can be. For archers and coaches alike, to notice changes in rhythm it is important to maintain historical video archives of technique. To notice drastic changes in rhythm, look at an archer at the beginning and the end of a year. To see smaller changes in his ability to dance with the bow, look at videos three months apart. In this way, anyone can begin to notice changes in control, fluidity, and the transitions between the various steps of rhythm.

FIGURE 14.4

Drawing a bow should be like trying to paint a beautiful
picture with long, smooth brush strokes. Some parts
of the painting require a little more finesse, and so
the brush strokes must slow down for the extra detail,
however blotchy pools of paint will form if the motions
are stopped altogether.

14 RHYTM

Invariably, all sports require rhythm. Merely completing a series of steps does not make someone an athlete, it means he is able to follow directions. Rhythm takes ingenuity, creativity, and harmony. To have rhythm, an athlete must be an artist. When a tennis player serves, he controls his rhythm with the height of his toss. If he tosses too softly, the ball spends less time in the air and the player must speed up his rhythm to strike the ball in time. If he tosses too strongly, the ball floats and the player must pause mid-windup. With the correct toss, not a second is hurried or wasted as the ball is struck swiftly and smoothly. Golf, too, has a similar concept. Should the athlete rush his backswing, he will be unable to control his loading, bending his elbow and losing control. Too slow of a backswing and he will likely jerk his downswing. The key in any sport, archery included, is repeating a process through the use of rhythm. Raising the bow and drawing must not only look the same each shot, it must last the same amount of time. Rushing through the loading position will leave an archer feeling weak for expansion. If he pauses too long, it will be too difficult to carry on with angular motion. When an archer's feeling begins to fade or become distorted under pressure, rhythm must be his guide to his technique.

Rhythm, next to timing (further explained in Chapter 24), is the second most important part of high-pressure match-play shooting. Even a very slight change in the time between loading and anchoring (from .5 seconds to .25 seconds) can completely change the shot, throw off the holding balance, and be the direct cause of a poor shot. Under high-pressure conditions, rhythm is hypercritical. It is also one of the last things an archer fits into his repertoire. First one must learn the steps of shooting, then he can learn how to blend them together. When in high-pressure matches, an archer can keep rhythm at the forefront of his mind because the step-by-step technique motions have become muscle memory in training. Even barring other mistakes, having good rhythm and timing in match-play conditions will invariably produce higher and more consistent scores than having good technique but poor rhythm and timing. As matches progress and the pressure builds, without rhythm and timing the archer's feeling of the other technique elements begins to quickly fall away. Perhaps he can shoot a good score for 12 arrows or maybe 24, but he will almost never win a championship.

Review

Rhythm dictates the elegance and fluidity of the shot. Using the angular motion learned in Chapter 10, coupled with drawing, Chapter 11, rhythm combines their concepts with body awareness and control (Chapter 25) to produce a beautiful shot. The fluidity and grace with which an archer draws a bow is that of the ballerina. Moving and drawing the bow should be like floating and gliding across the stage. There should never be anything staccato about an archer's movements. Shooting with smooth rhythm does not mean that the entire draw happens at the same speed. Quite the contrary: what classifies an archer at being smooth and fluid is his ability to blend together changes in speed and direction.

The key elements to remember about rhythm are:

• transitioning from drawing, through the loading and anchor positions, and past transfer, the archer should count, if silently, "oooonnneee, two, … threeeeee," to achieve the correct timing between the steps

• the step-by-step motions between set, setup, drawing, loading, and anchor are not observable in archers shooting with correct rhythm – everything is blended together

• by smoothly drawing the bow, archers will gain pinpoint clicker control, achieving a loading position less than three millimeters from the end of the arrow's point

• there is an inverse relationship between the speed at which the bow is drawn and the control used: when slowing down the drawing motions, more control should be used

• slight changes in rhythm can radically affect the confidence and control of the archer

Rhythm is more of a concept than it is a step, thus making it more difficult to practice than, for instance, the set position, where each of the body parts needs to be positioned just so. It will also take someone with a trained eye to notice small changes in rhythm. The best way to develop a greater sense of good rhythm is to watch videos of archery's highest competitions. The World Cup events and past Olympic competitions are easily obtained. Watching the world's best archers compete can only contribute to one's own grace and control.

Everyday All-the-time Archery

As time goes on, archery becomes more than something you do at the archery range. The mind of an archer becomes so fixated on technique and shooting that thoughts of archery creep into almost every facet of life. You might ride your bicycle and position your hand against the bars so you can feel the pressure point of the grip. While driving your car you might rotate your bow arm elbow down as if you were shooting. Archers across the world all develop little idiosyncrasies as archery becomes an important element of their lives.

Some favorite idiosyncrasies include grabbing grocery bags with three fingers as if holding the string, sitting in class or at work and pretend releasing a pen or pencil, and adopting the archery foot stance while taking a shower. If you don't do some of these things already, odds are you will soon. Already you probably notice how horribly archery is in many Hollywood movies – people shoot without tabs or finger guards, anchor against nothing somewhere back behind their ear, or shoot arrows that look like weeds. Likely you have been around people who also became excited when they heard you shoot archery, and have cringed at their poor form as they pantomime shooting. Archers notice such minor details.

Archery becomes part of you, and not just on the practice field. You grow special archery calluses on your fingers, and the middle fingers on your string hand become 30 percent larger than the same fingers on your bow hand. And odds are, if you shoot while wearing short sleeves, you have an armguard tan that looks more like a skin disease than something athletic. At the very least, it can be a good conversation starter.

Enjoy it. Breathe it in. Live the archery life. Live it everyday, all the time.

The mark of a full-time archer – the impossible to hide arm guard tan.

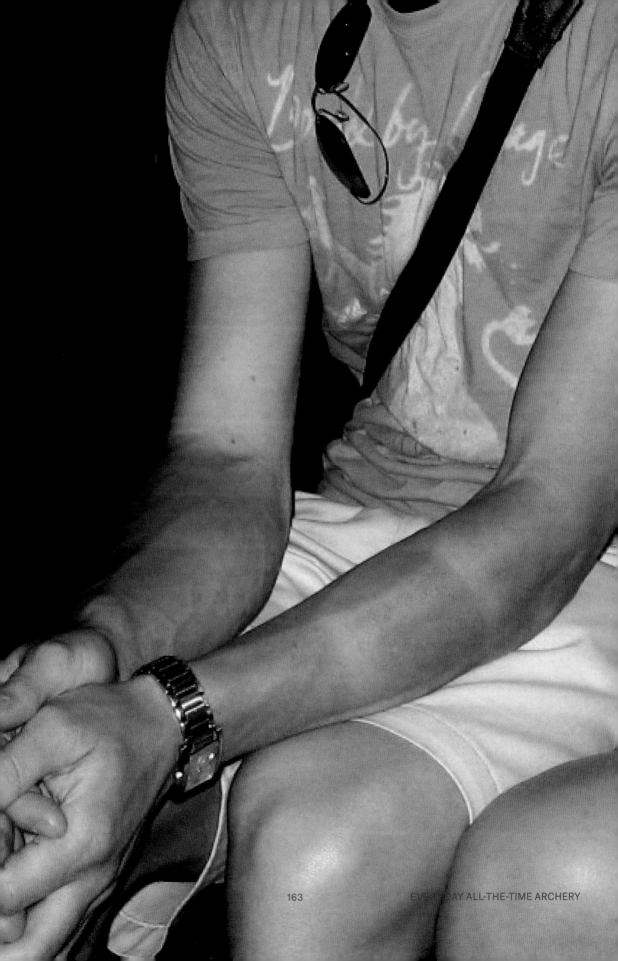

15 Transfer

Transfer is the final transferring of the holding intensity away from the arm and hands at the loading and anchor positions and into the back muscles.

Transfer is the third step of rhythm (see Chapter 14, "Rhythm"). The archer angularly directs the holding intensity through LAN 2 movement such that he is using the structure of his body to resist the force of the bow. This makes him ready to begin expansion and execution. It can help to think in terms of numbers, so imagine the archer holding 80 percent of the draw weight with his back muscles at the loading and anchor positions. He will therefore hold 20 percent with his fingers, hands, and arm. Next, to achieve the proper transfer position, the archer must transfer some of the holding force in the hands and arm into the back muscles. The correct ratio of balance at the holding position is 90 percent held with the back muscles, and 10 percent held with the hands and arms. It is not possible to transfer 100 percent to the back muscles because the fingers still need to hold onto the string and maintain their hook.

Without correct transfer, archers will invariably shoot a weak, collapsing shot that does not utilize the back muscles in a controlled and balanced manner. The result of linear techniques are forward releases and a general lack of consistency, control, and sense of calm. This is not to say that one cannot shoot very high scores with linear techniques, as many current world records were set in such a fashion, but it is unquestionably a technique of the past and soon all those records will fall to archers shooting the correct angular holding techniques.

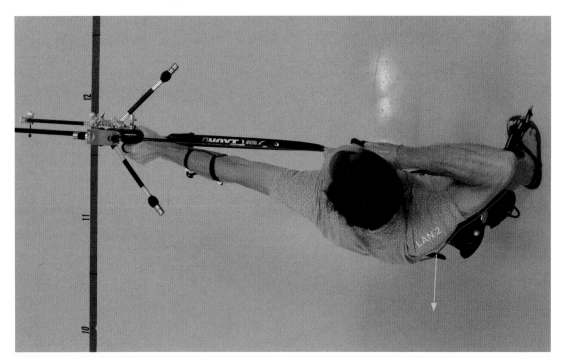

FIGURE 15.1 - Top view

The movement of the LAN 2 upon transfer is slightly down and parallel with the shooting line. See figure 15.2 for another dimension. From where the shoulder unit is in the photo, the transfer movement will move the shoulder unit until it lies at the red line. Transfer is then complete.

FIGURE 15.2 - Front view

Notice how the drawing shoulder is clearly visible. Upon transfer the archer should be able to read writing on his back in a mirror. The arrow depicting LAN 2 movement is pointing to the right and coming out of the picture, just barely down.

Though transfer is essentially a change in muscle intensity, it is achieved by a change in direction of drawing the bow. To think of transfer as a change in direction, instead of a change in muscle intensity, can prevent clenching, pinching, or breaks in rhythm. The concept of angular motion (see Chapter 10), should already be understood by this point. Drawing, loading, and anchor steps are not linear. Transfer, of course, is also angular. A very big misconception continues to plague many coaches and their archers: that only transfer is angular. Understand that while drawing, loading, and anchor are angular, transfer is characterized by torquing the drawing shoulder even further around the vertical pivot through the spine. See figure 15.3 and 15.4. Upon transfer, coaches should see no string movement in any direction on the archer's face, chest guard, or body. Transfer is a small rotation, not a pulling. Again, do not think of squeezing the back muscles tighter, as this will only build more tension and instability in the shot, decrease flexibility and cause loss of control. Instead, think of transfer as turning and changing direction.

Setup position   **Anchor position**   **Holding position – After transfer**

FIGURE 15.3

In these overhead views, pay close attention to the angle changes of the elbow. See how the scapula moves more out (to the left side of the picture) than it moves closer to the spine. The transfer motion is small and subtle to see, however it is noticeable to the trained eye. It is also easy to see the changes in position at the back of the drawing elbow. There is an easily noticed difference in elbow positioning between the anchor and holding positions, from 8 to 7 in the pictures. Also, notice how the front shoulder position and head position never change in any of the photos. Pay close attention to the lines that depict the instantaneous direction of the angular drawing motions. As we progress from

setup, through drawing, to the anchor and holding positions, it is easy to see the progression of the angular direction. If it helps, refer back to Chapter 10, "Angular Motion," which clearly depicts the understanding of instantaneous linear motion and its connection to angular motion. Notice how in the last photo it almost seems as though the archer's drawing forearm curves back around, somewhat like a banana. This is indicated by the yellow line. This position is possible due to a large amount of rotation that draws the elbow around, past the line of the arrow. The archer is now in the strongest position possible.

Think of transfer as stepping inside the bow, such that the archer is between the string and the grip, pushing outwards in both directions. When one is inside the bow, the archer can be said to have "stepped onto the chair." Stepping on the chair is a phrase used to describe the commitment of achieving transfer and holding techniques. It is a metaphor that covers both the change in mindset from the drawing, loading, and anchor steps, onto the chair, for transfer and holding, as well as the physical actions themselves. The change in direction from loading and anchor is also described – transfer is stepping in a new direction to step onto the chair. The metaphor can extend a step further to discuss sitting down in the chair such that one's feet do not touch the ground. This means that one is so committed to holding with his back, sitting comfortably in the chair, that he can relax and kick his feet as they are not needed to stay sitting – the archer can relax the arm, forearm, and hand, as they are not needed with correct holding technique.

Archers commonly make the mistake of moving too much to achieve transfer. During transfer, the hand and anchor positioning must stay exactly the same on the jaw. There must be no sliding whatsoever, and no changes in contact. The elbow will only move a tiny amount more around the body. Sometimes a very small amount of downward elbow movement can be noticed, however the archer should not attempt to create this motion. All of the focus must stay on moving around, not down. Everything from the shoulder all the way to the hand should look as if it were one piece, despite the fact there are three major joints joining them all. This means there should be zero change in any of the positions of the joints upon transfer.

Some archers can feel a very tiny sensation described as an opening of the chest due to the rotation of the drawing shoulder. This is only a secondary sensation and should not be concentrated on. In order to achieve transfer correctly every single shot, one must concentrate completely on turning through the shot and maintaining focus.

Loading position   **Anchor position**   **Holding position**

FIGURE 15.4

Again, notice the angle changes of the drawing elbow between loading, anchor, and holding position. As this is an oblique view, though vertical lines are drawn on the picture, changes in elbow position will actually correspond with a rotation, not a linear movement. Notice how the elbow position, depicted by the yellow circle, moves from line 5.5 at the loading position, to 4.7 at the anchor position, to 4.2 at the holding position.

This tells us a few things: angular motion must continue even between the loading and anchor positions, and the displacement of angular motion gets smaller the closer the archer gets to the holding position. Lastly, notice how the elevation of the elbow actually moves downward just slightly between the anchor and holding positions. This is caused by a natural turning of the shoulder with power coming from the low trapezius muscle.

Good angular direction

Good angular direction – Even more rotation than previous photo

FIGURE 15.5

The following two pictures both show good holding positions after transfer. Both of the drawing shoulders are rotated around such that the drawing elbow is directly behind the arrow, and even past the line of the arrow. Both archers are attempting to push their LAN 2 toward the left side of the page for expansion. The direction of the yellow lines is depicted by the height of the drawing elbow. As the archer in the top picture shoots with a relatively higher elbow position, the angle of his elbow to his shoulder is higher than the archer in the bottom picture. The direction of rotation should follow the line of the arm to the shoulder.

Many coaches will try to see transfer through scapular motion, as they wish to see it moving closer to the spine. While this movement can slightly be interpreted as correct, most coaches wish to see too much motion, and thus get their students to do more pinching and clenching, rather than the smooth transfer to holding. LAN 2 movement should precede scapular movement, making it the focus of transfer. Scapular movement between loading and anchor, and completing transfer, should be no more than one centimeter. While it is a small external motion, more importantly, it is an internal holding and shifting of force around the axis of rotation.

It is also very important to remember that transfer does not happen by itself. It must be made to happen every single shot, or it will not happen. One cannot step onto the chair if they do not lift their leg and move to step onto it. However, with sufficient practice, transfer will become more automatic. Muscle memory will begin to take over and it will feel like a normal and necessary part of the shot. It will only be during stressful competition that archers will have to consciously focus on transferring. Commitment becomes very important because archers must immediately begin to transfer after loading and anchoring as any hesitation will break the rhythm and the shot will be lost.

FIGURE 15.6

Here is another archer with great positioning after transfer. Her shoulder and elbow unit is strongly connected as can be seen by the elevation of the bottom of the drawing elbow joint and the elevation of the top of the scapula. Both positions are indicated in the photo. The direction of her expansion is indicated by the line of the backside of the drawing unit, in this case, depicted by the yellow arrow. Compare this to previous pictures in figure 15.5 and you will see some slight differences. All three of the pictures shown in figures 15.5 and 15.6 are acceptable positions.

Review

Once the safety has been switched off following the loading and anchor positions, transfer is akin to setting one's finger against the trigger and applying a bit of pressure, but not enough to make the gun fire. As learned from "Loading Position" (Chapter 12), the archer should already feel 90 percent ready to shoot the arrow upon correctly achieving the loading position. During transfer, the archer prepares himself the additional 10 percent. With successful transfer, then, the archer is in the 100 percent ready-fire position, poised on the edge of the clicker, where a slight expansion (Chapter 17) will displace the arrow through the clicker. It is of utmost important that angular direction (Chapter 10) is maintained during transfer. The archer should attempt to push his shoulder unit approximately perpendicular to his body to maintain angular motion, and parallel with the ground and shooting line. Re-examine figures 15.1 and 15.3 for clear pictures depicting correct LAN 2 movement and direction.

The key elements to remember about transfer are:

• transfer is a turning, led by the LAN 2, not a pinching or squeezing of the shoulder scapula muscles

• muscle intensity in the back muscles should always increase – there is never any relaxing that should be felt. The arm muscles might feel as though they are carrying less intensity, however the archer's focus should be on his back muscles, not his arm! Focus on the correct movement from the back muscles instead of trying to relax the muscles of the arm

• it is not possible to transfer 100 percent of the force to the back muscles because the fingers must maintain their full hook on the string

•the slight downwards direction of transfer should follow the line of the upper arm

• transfer is a mental state as well as a physical position: one must fully commit to taking transfer in order to actually do it

• should the elbow only dip or even move forward during transfer, the correct motion is not being achieved. Transfer is first and foremost a turning motion

• head positioning, hooking, and posture must remain absolutely still while transferring

• transfer is a small motion, exaggerated motion is detrimental to the shot

Transfer is like a sprinter priming himself in the starting blocks, waiting for the sound of the starter's pistol. His awareness is peaked, his intensity is strong yet controlled, and he is very much in the moment. Without transfer, it is impossible to achieve holding (Chapter 16), which is the cornerstone of controlled shooting. An archer that is not capable of comfortably holding his bow is not an archer that shoots with control.

16 Holding

Holding is defined as the body resisting the force of the bow through the use of controlled, angular drawing.

The position just after transfer, holding encompasses the expansion period, where the archer calmly and without shaking maintains the full draw position. Achieving the holding position is characterized by a smoothing of intensity as the bone structure of the body begins to resist the force of the bow. Muscles are not strong enough to achieve this task on their own. The holding position is often described as stepping inside the bow, where the archer is between the grip and string, pushing outwards in both directions, standing like Leonardo da Vinci's depiction of a man. Stepping inside the bow means the archer is more a part of the bow, inside it, and in alignment with it, rather than outside of the line of power, muscling and wrestling with its forces. As learned from Chapter 15, "Transfer," one must step on the chair to achieve the transfer, take the holding position, and stand inside the bow.

Though the holding position can be thought of as a calming, this is not to say any of the muscles relax. The holding position is chiefly characterized by having a low ratio of holding with the hands and arms to holding with the muscles of the back. The hands may be relaxing, but the back muscles are only increasing in intensity, and deepening their holding position. Think of the holding position like stretching the body. As one goes deeper and deeper into the stretch, certain muscles must calm and relax to allow the strong muscles creating the stretch to take over more and more. This same idea of going deeper into a stretch is how one goes deeper and deeper into holding.

FIGURE 16.1

When an archer has learned the finer points of holding he is capable of feats of strength that seem almost impossible. Here we see an archer practicing SPT with his competition bow and a stretch band adding an additional 15 pounds. With good conditioning and proper technique this archer can comfortably shoot 65+ pounds during drills.

FIGURE 16.2

Alignment is critical to proper holding. Here we can see the archer has his elbow past the line of the arrow, allowing him full access to the powerful muscles of his back. This archer has stepped inside the bow and is using his good alignment to resist the force of the bow purely with the bones of his body.

Holding can be practiced by doing 'specific physical training,' or SPT. Holding SPT is done by standing in front of a mirror, drawing the string, and reaching the holding position. For 30 seconds the holding position must be held. A large clock that counts the time in seconds is needed for this drill. After 30 seconds, the archer takes a minute rest. At the end of the minute, it is time to draw bow again and hold for another 30 seconds. The drill should be repeated for at least 20 minutes, and as the archer grows stronger, for up to an hour. Archers have done three or more hours of SPT without a break. This is a fast way to build more strength, familiarize the archer with the holding position, and teach him how to use the powerful muscles of the core and back to complete this drill. If an archer does not draw with angular motion and hold with the muscles of the back, he could never complete three hours of this drill. SPT is so important for an archer's progression that if one only has two hours to practice, breaking up the practice to complete an entire hour of SPT will give him far more benefit than simply shooting for the full two hours.

FIGURE 16.3

Viewed from almost directly behind, we can see that the elbow is actually past the line of the arrow, further around the head. Once the alignment is in such a position, it is far easier to achieve holding because the equal-opposite forces line up and oppose each other, rather than have opposite horizontal components that fight one another and threaten collapse.

FIGURE 16.4

Notice how the string is not touching the archer's chest guard. With correct posture and shoulder positioning, there is ample clearance for the string, bow arm, and chest. When the bow arm shoulder is not pushed with enough force toward the target, the string will creep closer and closer to the chest guard as the archer begins to lean on his heels more and more.

Review

Though most of the concepts of holding are prefaced by the techniques described in "Angular Motion" (Chapter 10), "Drawing" (Chapter 11), especially in "Loading Position" (Chapter 12), and in "Transfer" (Chapter 15), holding is a distinct position occurring after transfer has been achieved. Holding is impossible without correct alignment; correct alignment is only possible by drawing the bow angularly. The essence of holding is that the archer has drawn the bow angularly so that the point of his elbow is now completely behind the line of the arrow. The resulting alignment of joints produces the best bone-on-bone connection to lower demands on the musculature, because there is no horizontal force component created by the elbow being out of alignment with the arrow. All the same, even with impeccable alignment, it still takes a great deal of strength to hold a competition-weight bow at full draw for 30 seconds or more without shaking. The best technique in the world will still not get around the strength requirement that is only built up through hours of consistent training.

The key elements to remember about holding are:

• correct alignment of the drawing elbow completely behind the arrow is critical to a powerful holding position

• muscle intensity of the back muscles from the transfer must be maintained, or even increased, to keep the powerful holding position

• a lot of strength can be gained by doing SPT drills in front of a mirror – this can often be more beneficial than actually shooting arrows

• imaging going deeper and deeper into a stretch – the concept is much like going deeper and deeper into holding

• achieving the correct holding position is often described as 'stepping inside the bow'

The holding position is all about achieving the correct body alignment that makes holding the force of the bow the easiest. In this position, the body is now primed and prepared with excess energy to execute expansion (Chapter 17), the last technique element the archer has total control over. The correct alignment and force direction established at the holding position will dictate expansion, and, in turn, the release (Chapter 18), and the follow-through (Chapter 20).

17 Expansion

Expansion, the small internal turning and increase of holding intensity to displace the arrow through the clicker, determines the final direction and control of the shot before the arrow leaves the bow.

Succinctly put, expansion is the most important element of shooting because the most amount of control, care, and energy must be put into easing off the clicker with the correct holding, timing, and shot-balance. Many top archers around the world do not follow the steps of the other chapters, however every single one of them maintains perfect control and balance, if only through expansion. Put another way, one can do whatever he likes to get to full draw, and as long as he executes through expansion, he will shoot high scores. So why care about doing any of the other steps? Successful completion of the other steps will consistently place an archer within closer reach of achieving the holding balance, putting him in the most advantageous spot to complete expansion correctly.

This next sentence should be drilled time and time again into coach and archer alike: Expansion is the first part of the follow-through. The power and direction used in expansion will determine the strength, speed, and direction of the follow-through. As the string slips through the fingers upon the release, the force of the bow cannot be recaptured. The arrow, the bow, and the archer now obey all of the Newtonian force equations they built at full draw. Equal opposite force reactions dictate the direction of the bow jumping, the arrow flying toward the target, and the release hand/arm/shoulder unit snapping back along the neck. By giving a goal of what the follow-through should be, we now can figure out the required direction and intensity of expansion to achieve the desired outcome. The release and follow-through are reactions – they are not actions. Expansion is an action; in fact, it is the last action the archer completes, and thus the most important.

FIGURE 17.1

For expansion, the archer should only have a maximum of two millimeters of the arrow's point under the clicker. If the archer has more than two millimeters to expand, he no longer can only use internal movement to pop the clicker, resulting in a loss of control.

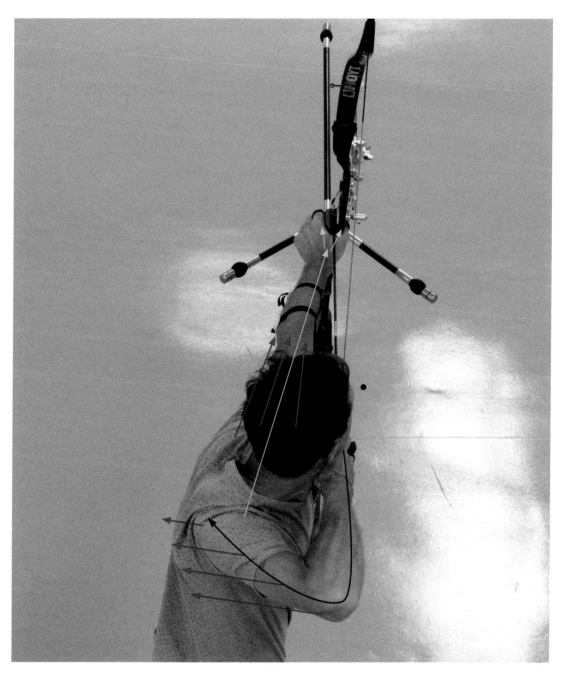

FIGURE 17.2

At the holding position, the drawing hand, arm, and shoulder function as one unit. We can see the shoulder alignment down the bow arm, and the pressure point through the bow hand, and out the bow hand thumb. For expansion, the archer increases his holding intensity along the force vectors shown by the red lines. Not much movement happens here as the archer should only be drawing 2-3mm through the clicker, resulting in only 1-1.5mm of movement in the front or back half of the shot, almost imperceptible externally. The archer should not be thinking to move or change alignment for expansion, as his focus should be on eye focus, aiming, and holding intensity. As blood pressure increases and holding intensity grows, focus on the balance of the front and back half of the shot, increasing intensity smoothly and with equal amounts. Archery is a sport of balance.

17 EXPANSION

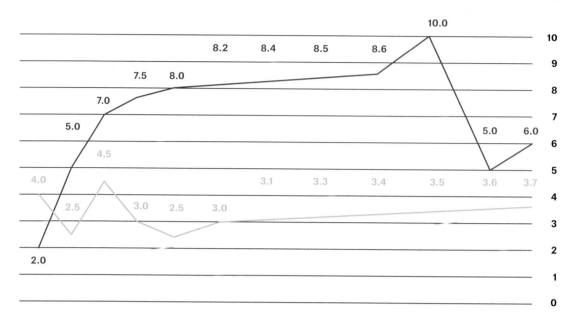

Raise bow	Setup	Draw	Load	Anchor	Transfer	Holding	Expansion 1 sec	Expansion 2 sec	Expansion 3 sec	Release	Follow - Through

FIGURE 17.3

This graph shows two very different ways of controlling intensity while drawing a bow. The yellow line shows the correct method of intensity control. The drawing motion has the most intensity (referring back to Chapter 14, "Rhythm," it also is the fastest part of the draw), however the intensity is quickly controlled at the loading and anchor positions. Following transfer, a very gradual, steady, controlled increase of intensity will result in proper execution at the moment of release, and a balanced shot. In the red line we see high intensities that clearly would result in shaking, loss of control, or a surprise forward release. Notice the smooth, even steps between the first and third second of expansion in the yellow line. Notice how the red line requires the archer to use all his intensity to displace the arrow through the clicker. Control and steadiness are the keys to successful expansion.

There are many details that make up the concept of expansion. The first, and most important, deals with the word expansion itself. When most of us think of expansion, we either think of a rubber band stretching, or of a balloon being blown up – something growing bigger – but the archer never experiences this type of expansion. Instead, the bow does. The bow is stretched taut, ready to be released, as it only must expand another millimeter before its energy will be loosed. Thus, the archer expands the bow just a tiny bit more and the arrow is released. But what does the archer do to make the bow expand? He cannot puff out his chest, expanding in the traditional definition of the word, to achieve this bow expansion. We see that expansion is a byproduct of another action, not the action itself. The action the archer must do is closer to a compression because the body tightens more to increase muscle intensity. Specifically, the shoulder and the LAN 2 continue their turning that they have been

FIGURE 17.4

In a good holding position, this archer will expand by pushing the LAN 2 parallel with the shooting line. Expansion should follow the slight downward slope of the drawing elbow to the LAN 2.

doing since the set position. To achieve expansion through the clicker, the archer must continue his angular motion, drawing through the body, not beside it. Visualize the angular motion of the shot pivoting around a vertical axis that goes through the spine. The body compresses inward on itself, it does not expand outward. If the string moves relative to the chest protector during expansion, the archer is expanding linearly. This makes sense because it means the drawing shoulder is extending, toward the drawing elbow, and away from the body.

It is possible to lose positioning on the clicker if the archer only concentrates on increasing his muscle intensity. Because he is just trying to flex his back muscles, he is not necessarily also causing the shoulder to rotate in the necessary angular motion to displace the arrow through the clicker. By clenching his back muscles the archer is likely only compressing himself, hence him losing clicker positioning. Very little LAN 2 and scapular movement is required to expand through the clicker because the drawing arm acts as a lever, increasing the actual displacement of the arrow proportionately. Angular movement must occur in conjunction with increases in muscle intensity for consistent expansion.

FIGURE 17.5

The muscles that control expansion are shown in the faint red outline. Focal points of intensity are denoted with the yellow circles. In this picture, the archer would press the force of his bow arm at his target (only intensity control, no visible movement takes place) while pushing the LAN 2 out of the page, toward the reader, for expansion. Synchronizing both sides of the shot is critical for a balanced release and follow-through.

First and foremost, the distance the arrow must travel is a critical element in figuring out what type of force the body must exert on the bow for expansion to take place. With the best approach, the arrow will only move a maximum of two millimeters during expansion. If the archer sets up farther than two millimeters away from the clicker, it is more difficult to control the force necessary to make the clicker go off. When an archer is struggling, he may have nearly the entire swage of the point to expand. It is the archer's job to draw, load, and transfer consistently so his expansion distance is always the same two millimeters.

Expansion is all about directional intensity control. On a scale of one to ten, one being totally relaxed and ten being shaking from the exertion, hopefully the archer is around a 3 or a 4 at full draw. Then, to expand, the archer must slowly and evenly increase his intensity with LAN 2 movement until the clicker goes off. Say the archer has an intensity of 3.5 at full draw and the clicker should go off around 4, the archer should increase his intensity, 3.5, 3.6, 3.7, and so on, until 4. Expanding 3.5, 3.5, 3.5, 3.7, 3.6, 3.9, 4.0 will result in wild and erratic shots because such a pattern does not have the control, balance, rhythm, and fluidity necessary for consistent expansion. The key is, not only must one arrow be shot correctly, but all the others after it have to be done exactly the same! One can also expand faster, starting 3.5, 3.7, 3.9, and so on, with the key and critical point being consistent increases in intensity. Many archers will stall, increase their intensity half of what is needed and hold there, eventually forcing the shot off with no control as their timing gets out of the optimum 2-3 second range of holding. Expansion intensity must be gradual, linear, and consistent.

As has been reiterated ad infinitum throughout this book, balanced shooting can only be accomplished by holding the force of the bow deep within the core and the strong muscles of the back. This same holding must be maintained and made even stronger during expansion. The control and balance of correct expansion comes from calm, controlled, and focused holding. There can be zero transfer back to the hands if the archer hopes to consistently repeat expansion shot after shot.

The direction of expansion is very important. Most archers intuitively try to expand along the jaw, even possibly allowing the string to slide along the jaw. However, this is a form of linear expansion, created by pulling the string with the arm, and not the internal rotation of the holding force that is needed. The string will not slide on the chin if expansion is done correctly. The direction of expansion should be felt through the head, not along the jaw. Remember, the rotation is around the spine. See figure 17.2 for a pictorial explanation of this concept. The LAN 2 drives expansion in the correct direction, not the draw hand.

The single-most repeated mistake, even when the archer knows better, is squeezing the fingers or hand to pull the last millimeter through the clicker. Distraction, fear of both success and failure, hesitation, and pressure will make an archer freeze with less than a millimeter to expand on the clicker. As the archer's intensity and anxiety of shooting the arrow builds but the clicker has yet to click, his body will begin searching throughout his body for more energy to expand through the clicker. Because the fingers are wrapped around the string, they are the first place the brain turns. Be it through actual squeezing, changing of finger pressure, or compressions of the hand or forearm, the brain loses the connection with the core and back muscles, resulting in collapsing, weak shots. It is next to impossible to replicate the small changes in finger pressure from shot to shot, and so it is an ill-advised method for expanding through the clicker.

Holding position

Follow-through position

FIGURE 17.6

Expansion is the first part of the follow-through. These two pictures are taken just moments apart, just before and just after the release. The red shape drawn on the first picture is a tracing of the arm position of the second photo. Especially so with the yellow line, we can see a very clear path the release hand must travel to finish at the follow-through position. It is along this direction that expansion must be felt. If the desire is to end up at the follow-through position, the direction shown in this diagram must be followed. It is helpful for all archers to capture their full draw and follow-through positions on camera, just as has been done here, and use before and after photos to get a clearer personal understanding of where the follow-through position is, and how expansion gets one to the follow-through position. The small red line on the white arrow represents how much the elbow has to move from the holding position to expand through the clicker.

After the transfer there needs to be a small amount of time, around a quarter to half a second, where the body settles the holding energy, preparing it for expansion. This is the time where the safety is switched off and now the archer is ready to fire. Prior to this safety getting switched off the clicker could accidentally go off but the archer would not release. Now that all the holding energies are balanced and the archer is physically and mentally prepared to shoot the arrow, expansion can begin. Expansion must be directionally oriented toward the final follow-through position, with consistent intensity increases and angular movement of the LAN 2. Hesitation cannot creep in and delay expansion as changes in rhythm and timing throw off the shot. Anxiety or fear creates hesitation. These emotions are felt the strongest during expansion because the archer intuitively knows the arrow will momentarily be in the air, and he will no longer be in control. The arrow always hits where it is pointed. Continued discussion on the anxiety and fear of shooting is carried out in Chapter 28, "The Emotionality of Shooting."

Review

Expansion is the final moment of control for the archer. Once his fingers begin to open for the release, the force and direction given by the back muscles will begin moving the arm backward off the string. Just as it is impossible to forcibly open one's fingers in time to release the string (see Chapter 18, "Release,") it is impossible to control the force and direction of the follow-through. The release and follow-through are a reaction of the force and direction of expansion. Expansion is the last controllable action of the archer. This is why it is so important. At full-draw and prepared to shoot, there is nothing more important for the archer to think about than the direction and intensity of his expansion.

The key elements to remember about expansion are:

• intensity control is very important for smooth expansion and must increase in a linear fashion from the holding position, all at as low an intensity as possible

• from the archer's full draw perspective of feeling, it is helpful to think of the direction of expansion as through the head. Expanding along the jaw would be unwanted linear motion, thus meaning the archer should feel as if he is squeezing his drawing hand tighter into his neck, the string pressing more into his face, as he completes expansion

• expansion is the first part of the follow-through

• expansion should occur by moving the LAN 2 approximately perpendicular to the plane of the arrow, parallel with the shooting line

• shot balance is everything: the bow arm must increase its intensity forward (though it is incapable of moving forward) as the drawing shoulder increases expansion intensity

Expansion plays the key role in timing (Chapter 24). Timing is the duration the archer spends on expansion, and completes the rhythm section (Chapter 14) of the draw. Any problems the archer had with any of the previous steps often manifest themselves in some way during expansion. Either it is too fast or too slow, does not have the correct direction, or lacks general control. Only with calm and consistent execution of the previous steps of shooting, especially drawing (Chapter 11), Loading Position (Chapter 12), anchor position (Chapter 13), and transfer (Chapter 15) can controlled expansion occur.

18 Release

The release,
described only as
the string slipping
out and around
the fingers, is the
critical last moment
when the archer
remains in contact
with the bow.

Much like the follow-through, the release is a non-action – it is a reaction. If finger pressure is maintained during expansion, holding intensity is controlled, and the body's power is held deep within the core, then the release will just happen when the clicker goes off. It is impossible to attempt to open the fingers in time to get out of the way of the string. High speed video analysis shows the string slipping through the fingers well before any active motion of opening the fingers is observed. The human body is not capable of reacting or moving fast enough to produce a mechanical type release, and it is silly to even attempt such a thing. The key to a good release is to relax only the tips of the fingers holding the string, allowing it to slip past the fingers, and not relax anything else.

FIGURE 18.1

We see the first archer just at the moment of release. Notice how his release hand is still against his face and the barrel of the gun is intact. It is very important to hold the power of the body all the way through the release to control the powerful forces.

Holding, just before the release   **⅟30th of a second after release**   **Approaching follow-through position**

FIGURE 18.2

These three photos show the angular nature of the release. The elbow, shoulder, and scapula unit move together as one, in the same direction as the holding force as dictated by expansion. The hand and fingers follow closely along the neck as the release force goes through the body, not beside it. In the second photo, notice how the fingers of the hand pull at the skin on the jaw and neck, maintaining tight contact well after the arrow is gone.

This relaxation of the finger tips does need to be practiced. Archers all around the world will unconsciously find themselves hooking their fingers around a finger on the opposite hand, holding for a moment, and releasing. Even something simple helps develop the muscle control necessary for a good release. Practicing with a heavy bucket, picking it up off the ground and letting it fall is another way to practice releases. This method allows the archer to feel the release, as well as visually observe it firsthand.

A good release looks as if nothing happened to the fingers holding the string. A moment before they were holding the string, and suddenly it is gone. The hook is still intact, the thumb is stretched back, the wrist stays bent outwards from hooking, and the anchor is still tight up against the jaw. The hand and fingers then stay in this position as the shoulder and arm unit snaps back due to the holding forces of the back muscles. None of the fingers open or pull up and away from the finger spacer. Literally, it should look as if nothing changed. The string should look as though it cut right through the fingers and came out the other side. This is the only way a release will appear sharp. Though the positions are maintained, all intensity in the hand that was used to hold the string must now have dissipated. Some archers may still retain tension in their hand throughout the follow-through, resulting in jerky, forced releases. A tense release may also be seen by fingers that flick out to the side or away from the finger spacer.

Holding, just before the release   **Release, ⅟30th second later**   **⅟30th after the moment of release**

 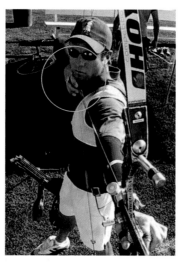 

FIGURE 18.3

This series of pictures showcases the moment of release, captured +/- ⅟30th of a second from the non-event. Pay close attention to the fingers, their lack of movement, and how similar the archer looks in the first and third pictures. The goal of the release is for the archer to remain the same after it has happened. While learning the release, it is helpful to the archer if he thinks, "There is no release. I never release the string. I cannot open my fingers fast enough to actually release the string." Think of the release as the string parting ways with the fingers, not the other way around. Eventually the release will become a subconscious element of the shot. During competition, an archer should never think of his release.

As we look deeper, a startling observation becomes apparent. There is no release! Because the holding intensity in the back keeps increasing, the archer should never concern himself with the release! The release is a reaction to the active holding and expansion energies and thus is an effect, not a cause. The second the archer starts imagining releasing the string, he will transfer his holding balance to the hands, causing forward releases and weak or inconsistent shots. The entire concentration of the archer needs to be on his holding intensity and direction, with an end goal of finishing at the follow-through position. The release is a reaction, happening somewhere between expansion and follow-through, but in the archer's consciousness it is a non-event, as it is not something he is actively capable of making happen.

As was explained in Chapter 17, "Expansion," the byproduct of forced expansion has archers squeezing their string fingers (at least slightly contracting their forearm/upper arm muscles) or changing finger pressure to expand through the clicker. Under duress to finish the shot, archers are unable to maintain their intensity and direction control, thus the squeezing of their fingers. This is not a technique element that many archers attempt to do, this is simply what happens when the archer begins to lose control. This mistake causes forward releases – active releases where the fingers open or fly outwards, breaking the angle of the wrist joint – or a flinging of the pinky finger. Video analysis, frame by frame at 30 frames per second will reveal the ailment. The top finger hook and finger pressure is most critical – it dictates the direction and control of the release. When finger pressure is held constant, the muscles of the forearm that hold the finger position are most ready to quickly relax, resulting in a clean release. If finger pressure is changing then the muscles are active. The archer must first stop his contractions and then release, resulting in a slower, less consistent release. Without consistent finger positioning and pressure, it is impossible to expand properly using the back muscles. Because the release is a reaction and not an action, errors of expansion will be revealed in the release. The release simply does whatever was dictated by expansion. It cannot be controlled. Completing correct holding and expansion is the only way a correct release can be executed.

The fingers of the release hand commonly strike the archer's neck as the hand goes flying past, somewhere around the larynx or just behind it. Some archers have even been known to bleed just from the leather on their finger tabs striking their necks shot after shot. Remember this is a reaction, not an action, so this is simply a way to observe a clean release. It is not advised to attempt to actively make the fingers hit the neck, but the thumb and fingers should slide smoothly past the neck and back around the head, maintaining contact with the skin the entire time.

FIGURE 18.4

This flyaway release has caused the string to hit the arm guard. Incorrect direction off the release throws off the follow-through, making the bow torque in the archer's hand. We can see the beginning of a correct bow hand release, however this hand provides only 50 percent of the direction off the string. As the release hand flies out to the right, clearly this will result in a lateral left force on the string, thus making it dangerous to the archer, and destructive to the shot.

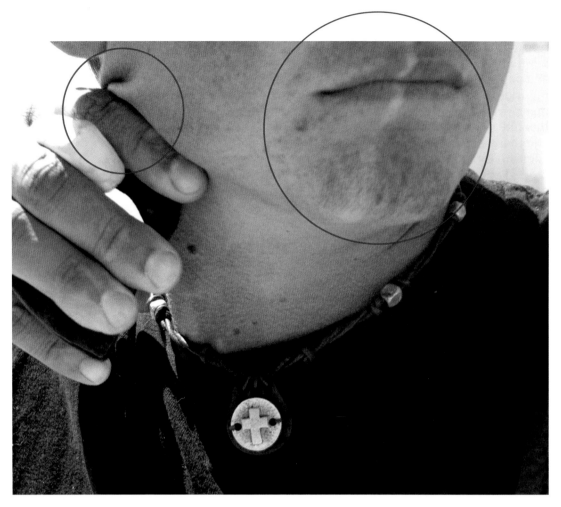

FIGURE 18.5

Here is a picture captured just after the moment of release. Notice the white line on the archer's chin and lips that signifies where the string was pushing tight against his face. Notice the bunched up skin at the back of the archer's neck. Even through the release he is expanding through his body. It is only possible to achieve this amount of contact through the release by not opening the fingers, expanding through the neck and head, and controlling intensity in the back muscles through the release.

The bow hand release must be synchronized with the string hand release. In order to balance the power of the shot, as the energy of the bow projects forward with the arrow, any remaining energy must be cast outside of the body with the bow hand release. Without synchronization of the two hands the body will have to absorb this energy, throwing off its balance, resulting in thrown bow arms, flyaway releases, and losses of body control. The essence of the release is characterized by the archer maintaining the balance of the shot and only relaxing the tips of his fingers, allowing the barrel of the gun and the core of his body to be the stable launching platform for the arrow. Considerable strength must be held within the body to keep the platform stable. The energy of the body has always come from deep within the core, and the strength must continue to be felt there.

FIGURE 18.6

Here is another photo that shows the archer just at the moment of release. Notice the lack of difference between the two photos, especially of the release hand.

Even while releasing the string the hand is still tight against the jaw, and the fingers are still curled as if holding the string.

The easiest way to tell if an archer is losing connection with his back just at the moment of release is to stand directly behind the archer and record video. Upon frame by frame analysis, the drawing elbow should show zero movement forward, up, or out, while the tensor muscles of the forearm begin to relax their grip on the string. Any possible movements will be very fast and only apparent in one or two frames, if recorded at 30 frames per second, however any movement in the directions described is the result of a collapsing shot. The best archers, even when viewed at 2000 frames per second, show no visible movement forward or out upon release. The release should travel in one fluid motion, slightly down, mostly back and around, to the follow-through position.

The release is a powerful motion, but it is not a jerking motion. It is sharp and cutting, but it is not forcefully sharp or cutting. A good release finishes softly while the powerful forces dissipate exponentially within the body and the archer moves to the follow-through position. If the forces are not correctly aligned at the holding position, then forced, jerking releases will result from the archer attempting to correct his mistake and still finish at the follow-through position.

Review

Release is a reaction, an uncontrollable event, and is best understood as an evaluation of, or judgement on, expansion (Chapter 17). If the body is controlled and expansion was executed correctly, the release will be beautiful. However, due to the extreme forces the body must control during expansion, coupled with the very small amount of movement during expansion, it is very difficult to critique problems by only analyzing expansion. The release amplifies any inconsistencies with expansion and makes it easier to diagnose critical lapses of technique.

A concept that must be drilled into all readers of this book is that the release must only come back off the string and must not ever move forward. If there is ever any forward movement of the elbow, the shot has collapsed.

The key elements to remember about the release are:

• the fingers cannot open in time to actively release the string – the string instead pushes its way through the relaxed, but still curled, fingers

• to achieve the best releases, it is best to only concentrate on the muscle intensity and angular direction of expansion and never imagine as though the release has occurred

• the top finger hooking position must be maintained during expansion and through the release for sharp, cutting releases

• in a successful release, the archer's fingers and hand never lose contact with his neck.

• the draw hand release must be synchronized with the bow hand release to balance out the jumping force of the bow

Many archers think the release is the most difficult thing about shooting. To counteract this idea, it helps to imagine as if the release never happens. All mental control and focus should be on the back muscle intensity and direction. When viewed from the perspective of the back muscles, there is no blip or loss of intensity at the moment of the release, making the release a non-event for the focused archer. Coupled with the bow hand release (Chapter 19), total balance of the releasing energies can be achieved while maintaining posture (Chapter 2) and body control (Chapter 25) past the follow-through.

Archery Games

To pass the time, all archers need some good archery games. Without an element of play, archery can get a bit boring. Of course safety first, which includes indigenous wildlife, but after that, let your imagination run wild! A little spontaneity can go a long way to making an endless practice feel like it is ending too quickly. A survey of archers was taken and the following are a few of their favorite games to play:

Lowest Arrow Pulls

This game needs at least two people, but the more the better. All archers shoot at a target (separate targets adds to the fun). It is best to play with at least six arrow ends, but again, the more arrows per end the better. Once all archers have emptied their quivers, a spotting scope is used to examine all the targets. Total score does not matter, as the entire premise of the game is the person with the single arrow farthest from the middle of the target has to pull everyone's arrows. The game gets particularly fun when all archers are of high skill level and the lowest scoring arrow might be a nine at 70 meters. The funny part of this game is when you goof up and shoot a six, announce it giddily to the group, and then someone else laughs at your poor shot and shoots a five.

Speed Shooting

Another community game, this one requires an agreed upon wager. All archers participating shoot 20-30 arrows as fast as they can at blank bale. The clicker must be used and no multiple arrows at a time! The slowest person is eliminated and the field is dwindled down until there is one man standing.

Tick-tack-toe

Much like regular tick-tack-toe, the same rules apply, however this is played at 70 meters. The target face is divided up into nine sectors of equal size with some tape, dark marker lines, etc. The catch of the game is that you have to call the square you are attempting to hit before you do so. If you land in another square, it doesn't count as a scoring arrow. First one with three in a row wins!

Sometimes you need to have a little fun.

19 Bow Hand Release

The bow hand release, sometimes referred to as the bow hand 'sit,' is the forward release of force caused by snapping the bow hand wrist in a downwards motion, balancing the powerful releasing forces of the draw hand coming off the string.

Without releasing the energy forward an archer will have to use extra strength to balance and control the force that remains until it dissipates in his body. Physics tells us it is easier to release the forward directed force by snapping the bow hand down rather than attempting to absorb and control it. It is not enough to relax the bow hand wrist on the shot as it does not balance the force of the string release hand. It must be very clear this is not a relaxed motion, the bow hand release should be forced as if casting something away from the body.

The first concept to embrace when attempting the bow hand release is to understand that even though the bow hand is snapping downwards, the bow arm must not drop. Though counterintuitive, snapping the bow hand down actually makes it easier to maintain the bow arm's position because it releases any unwanted energy forward – the arm does not have to absorb and control it. Most archers incorrectly apply considerable upwards force on the bow to maintain their bow arm position on the shot. To prove this claim to an archer, have them shoot without a finger sling and have someone in place to catch the falling bow. On the first shot the bow will drop, the archer's arm will fly upwards, and his body will rock backwards and out of balance. This forces the body to absorb the energy that should be correctly dissipated through the bow hand release. With practice the archer will be able to snap his hand down and keep his bow arm up, and without a finger sling. After the archer has successfully accomplished this task, he is ready to repeat the same drill with a finger sling.

FIGURE 19.1

This is the hand positioning just before the clicker going off. Notice how the index finger points down at the ground, providing direction for the release. The thumb is spread out and maintains a constant force holding it straight. The thumb appears curled, but this is only because the archer is holding intensity in it to keep it in position.

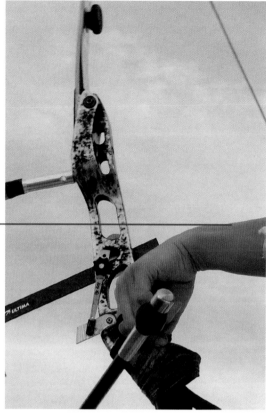

FIGURE 19.2

As the bow begins to jump forward, the bow hand must snap down to release the forward energy of the bow. See how the bow arm position is maintained, and only the wrist has moved. The index finger should be along the side of the bow, pointing down at the ground. Notice how the wrist is not curled inward, it only points straight down at the ground. Also see how the bow arm has still maintained its elbow rotation-this means the triceps muscle is still tight and pushing toward the target. The archer should work to keep his hand spread wide, even during the bow hand release, as this will provide the best force and direction.

To achieve a good snap, it is very important to maintain the pressure point low in the bow hand and low in the grip. This, too, is counterintuitive, because it is easy to imagine how pushing higher in the grip would allow the hand to snap faster because it has a shorter range of motion. Instead, pushing high in the grip only leads to the wrist moving forward on the shot, not in the desired downward motion. The lower pressure point position, coupled with full, firm contact throughout the bow grip (see figure 5.2), create a stronger and more stable brace against the force of the bow, allowing the forward force of the string to cast the bow forward with minimal energy loss, thus freeing the hand to direct the force downward and into the finger sling while the bow is jumping out of the hand. If the pressure point shifts higher in the hand and toward the throat of the grip, the arm and wrist will be inclined to move upward upon release.

19 BOW HAND RELEASE

Correct

Incorrect

FIGURE 19.3

Look at the contrast between these two photos. In the top photo, the bow arm stays straight to the target while the wrist projects the force of the bow forward, out, and down. In the picture on the bottom the archer does not release with the bow hand wrist – see how the bow arm is consequently pulled down with the weight and inertia of the jumping bow. In the bottom photo, the bow is controlling the archer, pulling her arm, fingers, and wrist out and down. In the top photo it is easy to see the control of the archer as even his thumb remains flexed and directed.

It is important to maintain the distance between the thumb and forefinger during the bow hand release. As is outlined in Chapter 5, "Grip Positioning," the bow hand should be spread between the thumb and pinky fingers. The same amount of spreading of the hand needs to be maintained during the bow hand release because it keeps the stable foundation necessary for the bow to jump forward. Also, archers may pinch the bow if the finger spread is not maintained, torquing its direction and throwing off the shot.

The finger sling plays an important role in the bow hand release because it catches the bow as it jumps out of the hand. If there is too small or too large a gap between the hand and the bow, the jumping forces will not be controllable. The optimum distance for the bow to jump is between 1 to 1.5 inches (2.54 cm - 3.81 cm), measured as the distance between the web of the hand between the thumb and forefinger and the throat of the bow grip. This distance should be checked prior to shooting the bow by just pulling the bow hand back from the grip until the finger sling is taut. If the bow does not have enough distance to jump, the powerful forward force of the bow can pull the archer off balance or create a shocking sensation through his arm. If the sling is too long, the bow will jump out, lose direction and momentum, and then hit the finger sling, providing the archer with weak, inconsistent, or incorrect feedback. Most archers with incorrect finger sling sizes tend to err on the long side. Other types of bow or wrist slings do not allow the wrist to snap down as normal, do not provide as direct or helpful of feedback to the archer, and are not suggested for use.

Use the index finger as the main source of direction for the bow hand release. While at full draw, the index finger should be pointing toward the ground and can be used as the force alignment for the bow hand release. During the release, the index finger should move along this line and end up pointing back at the archer's feet. The entire bow hand release is one fluid, downward, snapping motion. See figure 19.2 for before and after examples of an archer completing the bow hand release.

It is very common for the archer to curl his wrist inward so the palm of the hand is visible to the archer – this is not the correct direction of force. Successfully completed, the palm of the hand should be hidden from the archer's sight by the bow arm wrist; the index finger should be visible pointing straight down to the ground. It is incorrect if neither the palm nor the index finger is visible because they are blocked from view by the bow arm. Providing correct direction is very critical to the successful completion of the bow hand release.

FIGURE 19.4

This archer is particularly fun to watch because she has such a forceful bow hand release that her bow catapults out of her hand and spins around backwards during her follow-through. Notice how her bow arm positioning is maintained even though her bow hand is now pointing back at her body. Some archers are able to get their bows to rotate like this, however it is not mandatory for shooting.

Review

The bow hand release controls the forward force and direction of the releasing force of the bow. Pressure point and grip positioning (Chapter 5) in the bow hand predetermine much of what happens for the bow hand release. By directing the force of the bow out and forward at the target, the bow hand release balances out the powerful backwards release of the string hand. Without the bow hand release, the balance of the shot is lost and direction will be inconsistent.

The key elements to remember about the bow hand release are:

• the index finger must snap down toward the ground at the moment of release to cast the bow out and forward

• the bow hand should move independently of the bow arm, isolating all the movement to the bow hand wrist

• the thumb and forefinger must maintain their lateral spacing so as to not pinch the bow while it is jumping out of the hand

• the triceps muscle must maintain intensity to keep the bow arm strong during the bow hand release

• a low and powerful pressure point provides the most snap for the bow hand release

• a finger sling that is too long or too short will give incorrect feedback to the archer. The optimum distance is between 1 to 1.5 inches (2.54 cm - 3.81 cm)

• the best way to learn the bow hand release is to shoot without a sling and have a coach catch the bow as it falls to the ground

A good bow hand release is necessary to balance out the expelled energy of the release (Chapter 18). Without balance and control, the archer will not be able to maintain performance and consistency. A common symptom of a poor bow hand release is a bow arm that is pulled downward by the bow when it hits the finger sling. Remember, the bow hand release is a forced motion – it will not happen without action by the archer.

20 Follow-through

————

Follow-through, the balanced finishing of the holding energies post-release, is a reaction of the force and direction of expansion.

Only a controlled archer can finish his shot with the clean snapping and breaking that is recognizable in Olympic champions. Since the follow-through is an extension of the moment of release, its successful completion is dependent on the execution of the action that causes the release: the holding and expansion phases of the shot. All sports concern themselves with a follow-through because the powerful forces generated by 'finishing the shot' need to be balanced, directed, and controlled through their release. For golf, this means holding the intensity within the core such that the athlete stays balanced on his feet, allowing his arms to smoothly wrap around his head. Upper body stability is created by a strong lower body that maintains its power and direction through the follow-through. For a baseball pitcher, this means crunching at the abdomen to pull the force of the body down, forcing the trailing rear foot to fly around and over the head while the chest and shoulders rotate through the target.

FIGURE 20.1

This archer has a beautiful, balanced follow-through. Notice how there is almost a straight line from his bow arm wrist to the back of his drawing elbow. Newton's third law, of equal and opposite reaction, is preserved as this archer uses good direction during expansion to ensure a calm follow-through position.

FIGURE 20.2

The barrel of the gun must be maintained throughout the entire follow-through. It cannot change between holding and the final follow-through position. This is the only way the follow-through can be executed.

Archery is no different than other sports. To learn how to achieve a beautiful archery follow-through, watch a PGA professional hit a drive from the far tee boxes or observe a Cy Young winner deliver a signature curve ball. Archers, too, require a controlled finish of the body's exertions. Because every movement has an equal and opposite reaction, the only things that should move during the follow-through of an archer is the bow-hand snapping down and the drawing hand/shoulder/scapula release unit snapping with equal force back around behind the head. Any other motion is extraneous, and will adversely affect the shot. If the release hand goes up, down, or transversely along the jaw, the archer has made an equal and opposite error before release. The force must travel through the head, with no wavering of direction backwards and rotationally off the string.

FIGURE 20.3

Here we can clearly see the path the elbow travels to reach the follow-through position. The total vertical distance the elbow travels is shown with the green line between both photos, as well as the yellow vertical line showing the exact distance. It is OK if the elbow moves down this amount, however should the downward motion begin to look more prominent than the rotational movement around the head, then something is going wrong during expansion/release. This archer also demonstrates picture perfect head and body control through the release.

It is best to think of the follow-through as a final position, rather than as the motion to get to that final position. One should use a snapshot of an archer like the one in figure 20.1 and visualize this picture in his head as the end goal. Chapter 17, on expansion, taught us that "expansion is the first part of the follow-through." This means, with a clear idea on where the follow-through should finish, the power and direction for expansion can now be determined. Getting to the follow-through position requires a long motion – expansion is just the first two millimeters of that motion.

The hardest part of the follow-through is to maintain the holding intensity, or even increase it, when approaching the final follow-through position. The body naturally wants to release and relax everything when the string begins to release through the fingers. This is what happens on a collapse. To achieve the correct, balanced follow-through, the core strength must be maintained, the triceps muscle in the bow arm must continue pressing toward the target, and the back muscles on the drawing side must sustain their holding. Just like drawing, loading, transfer, and expansion, the follow-through is angular, both in intensity and direction. Even a slight loss of intensity during the follow-through may break the shot, cause the archer to lose feeling, or cause a total collapse.

FIGURE 20.4

Here is another example of a good follow-through position. The archer's bow arm is directed at the target, complete with a beautiful bow hand release snapping down at the ground. Eye focus is held on the aiming point, the release hand and arm has traveled angularly behind his head, and the archer's face remains a picture of calm. It is easy to feel the concentrated energy of the archer through this photo.

FIGURE 20.5

It is helpful for the archer to learn his follow-through position by closing his eyes while shooting. Without visual distraction, the archer will be able to achieve a better sense of power and feeling.

The key component of executing a good follow-through is maintaining the barrel of the gun. As seen from above in figure 20.2, the barrel of the gun starts at the drawing shoulder and extends through the front shoulder, out the bow arm, and into the bow. Upon release, extending to the follow-through, this exact alignment must be maintained, or the shot is broken. The barrel of the gun is the launching platform for the arrow and must remain rigid. Should the line be broken, (the drawing shoulder collapsing inwards or the bow shoulder collapsing outwards), the launching platform will have become weakened. The archer will no longer have consistent direction, and the arrow will be errantly cast. Keeping the barrel of the gun is very difficult to do because the brain has difficulty relaxing only the fingers as the string releases. A break may only last 1/10th of a second, however this encompasses the entire launching of the arrow from the bow. Archers can practice this technique by shooting with a rigid Form Master™ or Shot Trainer™. These training devices attach to the bow string, wrapping around the drawing elbow, and connects the archer to the string at the moment of release. Should the archer lose his back muscle holding intensity at the moment of release, his arm will be jerked forward under the 50 pounds of force from the string.

The drawing hand, wrist, elbow, arm, shoulder, and scapula should work and move as one. It is easy for the drawing force to explode through the joints connecting these body parts (there are many, thus large room for error), breaking the connections and causing inconsistency. The archer must use technique to control his force and exertions, making everything move as one piece. Maintaining the barrel of the gun depends on these connections.

Review

The follow-through position is a result of the intensity and direction of expansion. Though the follow-through involves motion, to think about it as a position is helpful because it gives the archer a fixed image to concentrate on. When the goal of expansion is to reach the follow-through position, the archer has determination and direction.

Intensity control and directional shot balance are the important keys of the follow-through position. The balance does not specifically refer to balancing on one's feet, but instead the balance of the forces of the shot. The release (Chapter 18) and the bow hand release (Chapter 19) must be synchronized to balance their equal and opposite directions and torques. If the torques are not balanced, the body will jerk or sway in the direction of the more powerful force.

The key elements to remember about the follow-through are:

• the key to achieving a smooth follow-through is to concentrate on the final desired position, and then make the most direct path to that position from holding

• shoulder alignment must be preserved through the release and the duration of the follow-through: should position change, the torques are not balanced between the bow arm and the drawing shoulder

• head position and posture must remain constant throughout the follow-through

• keeping the source of the body's power deep in the abdomen will help control any excess forces that might otherwise have caused the body to move or lose control

• as long as rotation off the string remains constant, the farther the drawing elbow wraps around the body during follow-through, the better: a long, strong, powerful follow-through is a result of strong, determined, and constant expansion

Much like the release, the follow-through is a diagnosis tool to examine what might have gone wrong earlier in the shot. Should head position change during drawing, the head will likely jerk at the moment of release. If shoulder alignment is incorrect or the holding position is never reached, the draw elbow will not power smoothly off the string and back around the head. An archer with good feel will begin to be able to notice smaller and smaller differences or shifts of position while reaching the follow-through position. Practicing on holding everything still will help the archer calm his body and eliminate any excess motion.

21 Shoulder Alignment

___

As its name suggests, shoulder alignment defines the direction of the shoulders in relation to the target. Paradoxically, the shoulder alignment should not be directed at the target.

While this seems like a good idea, it does not take into account the drawing elbow positioning relative to the shoulder alignment or the biomechanical workings of the shoulder. In actuality, the direction of the line indicating the alignment of the shoulders should point well past the target. For right handed archers, the line should be 15-20 degrees past the target to the right, and for left handed archers the line should be 15-20 degrees to the left. The elbow, the true direction of force off the string, must rotate into alignment with the arrow through angular drawing. This leaves the shoulders in the strongest biomechanical positioning for holding.

To achieve correct shoulder alignment the set position, (Chapter 8), drawing, (Chapter 11), and transfer, (Chapter 15), must all be executed correctly. While correct shoulder alignment with proper control is the goal of these steps, it is not an actual step itself. The archer must achieve shoulder alignment through the steps, not separately or as an additional motion.

FIGURE 21.1

The line of the arrow is marked with the red line. Notice how the shoulder alignment is pointing across the line of the arrow. This is the biomechanically strongest position for holding the forces of the bow.

Setup position shoulder alignment   **Holding position shoulder alignment**

FIGURE 21.2

At the setup position the shoulder alignment still looks similar to the alignment at the holding position. In the first photo on the left, the archer would just be able to read the USA on his back if he were shooting toward a mirror. The yellow line represents the shoulder alignment from the drawing shoulder through the bow arm shoulder, and down the bow arm. The red line represents the line of the arrow. In the first photo, notice how the red line angles to the left of the target. This is good positioning because as the archer draws with angular motion, the red line will swing more to the right to come in direct alignment with the target. If the archer attempted to keep the arrow pointed straight at the target from the outset, he could not draw with angular

motion. In the photo on the right, notice how the yellow line is now pointing even farther to the right while the red arrow has come around to point at the target. The faint lines on the second photo represent the exact positions of the lines from the first photo. These photos also show fantastic rotation of the shoulder between the setup and holding positions. In the left photo, notice the green line drawn over the seam of the shirt. In the photo on the right, the faint green line represents the exact location of the seam from the first photo, and the green arrow shows the extent of rotation that has occurred. Also notice that one can almost read the entire USA on the archer's back at the setup position – at the holding position only half of the A is still visible.

FIGURE 21.3

Here we see an archer working on his alignment by using a form strap. As the strap is rigid, it isometrically teaches the body to conform and contort to the new positioning. This drill is the best way to learn how to compress the body and achieve better shoulder alignment without changing the draw length. Practicing this drill stretches the body and changes feeling while achieving greater ranges of archery-specific shoulder flexibility.

Shooting archery requires angular motion to launch a linear projectile. The shoulders work on rotation, not extension, so it impossible for the shoulders to produce power in a linear direction, as was explained in Chapters 10 and 11, "Angular Motion" and "Drawing." This concept is easily recognized in small oil derricks or the common piston engine. A small displacement of angular motion moves a shaft up and down to produce power over a long linear displacement. The shoulder works much the same as these engines. Connected to a long rod – the arm – the shoulder rotates internally to produce linear displacement of the arrow.

The best way to see, learn, and change incorrect alignment is to draw back a stretch band or a light bow in front of a mirror. By standing directly in front of a mirror, the archer is able to see all of the relative positions of the joints. He can observe what the changes he feels in his technique look like from a third person point of view. At the set position, the front shoulder should appear pushed down to the ground and toward the target. The drawing shoulder should just barely peak out behind the front shoulder such that the archer could almost read his name if it was written on the back of his shirt. At the setup position, the turning of the shoulder is only more noticeable, as slightly more of the drawing shoulder can be seen in the mirror. Drawing to the loading position rotates the shoulder even more, and, of course, transfer and expansion are also angular. At the holding position the archer should clearly be able to see his drawing shoulder in the mirror.

Shoulder alignment is also learned by using a nylon strap, sometimes called a form strap, that has a length that is one inch shorter than the full draw position. A nylon strap is necessary because it is very resistant to stretching and lets the archer practice isometrics. Have the archer stand in front of a mirror as outlined before, and draw the strap to its full length. Achieving the correct shoulder alignment is achieved through an internal turning and compressing, not by pulling and extending. A great deal of force should be applied to the strap. The archer should attempt to turn his shoulder with more power and direction than what he feels is necessary. This is also a great warmup technique for shooting, as an archer can apply 80, 90, or 100 pounds of force against the strap to wake up the muscles, stretch and compress the body where necessary, and prepare himself for the correct shoulder alignment and positioning of shooting.

Archers often make the mistake of pushing or rolling their front shoulders in toward the string in an attempt to push shoulder alignment even farther to the right of the target. Their notion is incorrect and can lead to difficulties with clearance, the string hitting the armguard, or violent breaking of the shot upon release. As we learned from Chapter 7, "Bow arm," at no time should the bow arm push in any direction except straight at the target. It is impossible to swing the drawing shoulder further around and behind the front shoulder by pushing the front shoulder in toward the string.

FIGURE 21.4

The front scapula position is marked in yellow and the rear scapula position is marked in red. Notice how the red shape is significantly lower than the yellow. The lower scapula positioning allows the drawing shoulder to use the powerful muscles deep within the back while the front shoulder uses the energy of the triceps, marked in green.

When the correct shoulder alignment and force is held within the muscles of the back, the shot will break cleanly 50/50, forward to the target and angularly back around the body. This clean breaking is created by the biomechanically correct shoulder positioning and strong muscle intensity.

Last, it should be noted that the drawing scapula should be slightly lower than the bow arm scapula. The positioning is a product of angular drawing; the intensity is stored during loading and then held during anchoring and transfer. With the drawing scapula lower than the bow arm scapula, there is extra room for rotation because the scapula points are not squeezing together. The scapula will wing outward away from the body, because this is the direction of the holding force. A winging scapula is one that sticks out away from the body, as is seen in many of the photos in this book when the featured archer is not wearing a shirt.

FIGURE 21.5

Here we can see the direction of the arrow at the target as indicated by the stabilizer. Look at the drastic difference between the arrow line and the shoulder alignment. This picture is especially nice as it looks right down the shoulder alignment, sharply contrasting the two angles.

Review

Shoulder alignment could be thought of as the foundation alignment for the rest of the shot. Though the actual force alignment is through the arrow, drawing fingers, and elbow, the shoulders control where the elbow alignment lies. If proper rotation of the drawing shoulder is not accomplished through angular drawing (Chapter 11), then it will be impossible to draw the elbow completely around behind the arrow. Of course, the elbow alignment could be affected by other difficulties with anchor or draw hand positions, but it is the shoulders that predominantly control elbow positioning. To achieve the correct elbow positioning completely behind the arrow, the shoulders must point well past the line of the target, as indicated by many photos throughout this book.

Achieving proper alignment while holding a competition weight bow requires great strength to torque the drawing shoulder around. SPT holding training or exercises done with a rigid nylon form strap can help the archer to learn the correct position.

The key elements to remember about shoulder alignment are:

• shoulder alignment must point well past the line of the arrow (to the right of the target) to achieve a good holding position where the drawing elbow is completely behind the arrow

• shoulder alignment must be preserved through the release and follow-through. Should position change, the torques are not balanced between the bow arm and the drawing shoulder

• the front shoulder should push forward toward the target as far as possible to create room for the drawing shoulder to rotate sufficiently and comfortably around the spine

• better shoulder alignment is best learned with a rigid nylon form strap that allows the archer to twist his body without changing draw length

• as long as rotation off the string remains constant, the farther the drawing elbow wraps around the body during follow-through, the better: a long, strong, powerful follow-through is the result of strong, determined, and constant expansion

Shoulder alignment is closely related to the set and setup positions (Chapters 8 and 9). Shoulder alignment then works directly with angular motion (Chapter 10), because the alignment of the shoulders change angularly during drawing (Chapter 11). With correct shoulder alignment, a good holding position can be achieved (Chapter 16).

Practicing in All Conditions

If possible, practice in warm, calm, and comfortable conditions. Many archers take a macho stance on this subject and end up making a potential problem worse by practicing in hurricane-like wind. Clearly, it is impossible to shoot consistent shots in such conditions. By no means is this an argument for never practicing in anything other than weather bliss. It is very important to understand that no matter the conditions, you can still shoot your shot. The point is, archery is a sport of repetition. The more times you can shoot your shot and have it feel comfortable, controlled, and smooth, the greater reserve of feeling you will have. Inconsistent practice, where each arrow is shot differently because the wind is blowing you around like crazy, will often only make feeling good shots that much harder.

Sadly, we do not all live in perfectly temperate climates. The whole reason that many places have an indoor season is because it is too cold to practice outside! There are many archers who quickly prepare for outdoor season the week before their first big competition outside. One week of shooting outdoors in the snow is generally enough for most people. But the truth is, sometimes it is good to push beyond your comfort zone. It takes out all the possible excuses you may have for why you did not perform very well – and that is a good thing. You may not like shooting in the rain, but if you have practiced it a few times and have been able to prove to yourself that you can still hit the middle just the same as always, then it surely cannot be different if it rains during a competition. Likewise, cold, stiff fingers are never fun to shoot with, but it's OK to prove to yourself a few times a year that you can still shoot no matter the conditions. Just don't go seeking self-punishment. Archery is hard enough already, don't try to make it even harder.

Shooting in the cold can be no fun, but sometimes it is necessary. Clothing is the name of the game. It must be fitted, wind-stopping, and, most importantly, warm. Though accuracy drops, even gloves can be worn if it gets too cold.

22 Breathing

Breathing is the rhythmic inhaling and exhaling of a percentage of an archer's total breathing capacity in organized conjunction with the execution of technique elements.

Breathing is the single best source of establishing a rhythm in the shot as it calms the body and provides natural rhythm. It helps the steps of drawing a bow to be deeper and more controlled. Breathing ties together all the complicated motions of shooting and makes them beautiful. Besides, you die if you don't do it!

An archer must breathe like a singer and control his breath with the diaphragm. For those not familiar with this type of breathing, start out by lying down on the floor, facing upwards. To breathe with the diaphragm, breathe through the nose so only the stomach rises on the inhales, not the chest. With total diaphragmatic breathing, the chest will not rise or fall. It helps to gently rest the hand on the stomach to feel the diaphragm expand and contract. To breathe in, push the hand up with the stomach. All of the breathing should be done through the nose as it is more calming and allows for greater control.

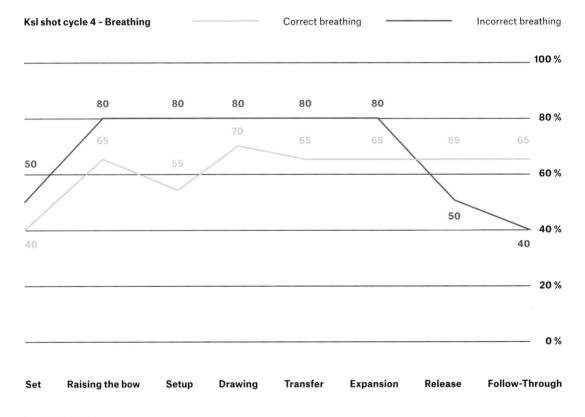

Ksl shot cycle 4 – Breathing   Correct breathing   Incorrect breathing

FIGURE 22.1

This graph shows two examples of breathing while shooting, one correct and one not. In the incorrect example notice how after raising the bow the archer holds his breath the remainder of the time. This builds up tension and does not help the body to flow. Also, the breath is released at the moment of release, resulting in a weak shot. The line of the correct example flows gently up and down, hovering a little above half capacity of the lungs. The breath is let out when the shoulders need to settle lower into the body and is held when the greatest control is needed. After the shot is released the breath can be let out after the follow-through in a natural and calm expulsion.

Breathing should never use up the total capacity of the lungs. It actually takes great strength to fill the lungs to maximum capacity. Likewise, it is equally difficult to completely expel all the air from the lungs. The greatest control is possible around a more medium amount of breath. During normal speaking, a person only fluctuates between 40 percent and 60 percent lung capacity. Breathing moderately, 70-80 percent will give the body the greatest amount of available strength. Before raising up the bow the lungs should be approximately at 40 percent capacity.

Breathing in while raising the bow fills the body with energy and fresh oxygen for the shot. Breathing out slightly at the setup position helps set the bow arm down and out and keeps the chest down and power low in the abdomen. Breathing in while drawing helps fill the body with energy and fresh oxygen again during the largest movement. Breathing out a very small amount again at transfer helps to settle and calm the body, preparing it for the final execution. One or two seconds after the follow-through the archer can breathe normally while preparing for the next shot.

FIGURE 22.2

The breath must be held at full draw to steady and control the body.

FIGURE 22.3

Above we see a group of archers working on relaxation techniques through controlled breathing exercises. Many top level archers practice breathing techniques up to an hour a day in conjunction with a full day of shooting.

Most archers will even adopt a breathing pattern for walking to the line, loading arrows, and resting between shots. This helps to complete all the steps in the same amount of time. Calm, slow breathing helps to control anxiety and relax the body between arrows.

Breathing is also very important while shooting because it provides the best way to control anxiety during pressure situations. A few deep, controlled breaths can lower the heart rate, dissipate adrenaline, and relax tense muscles. Many archers use a variety of breathing/relaxation training to supplement their shooting. Examples include guided meditation, yoga, and focused controlled breathing. With plenty of practice an archer is able to achieve similar relaxation while shooting as he achieves in his yoga classes. The one simple lesson learned from breathing training is that after 30 seconds of very deep, slow breathing (in for six seconds, out for six seconds), the blood is filled with more oxygen than normal, eyesight slightly improves, and the muscles have plenty of energy available for work. Though these effects wear off in a few minutes, this technique can be used prior to stressful matches when the archer needs any advantage he can get. Over time, this deep breathing will become a routine and will help the archer find his center of calm and relax.

Review

Archery is a meditative art that requires enormous concentration and control. Like many other art forms that require similar control, breathing becomes the focus of the heart and mind to maintain the calm necessary for absolute precision. Diaphragmatic breathing is used in everything from singing to weightlifting and yoga, where control, power, and concentration is needed. Archery is no different from these other art forms, because a steady, controlled, repeatable breathing pattern is necessary for mastery of skill.

The key elements to remember about breathing are:

• breathing should never use the maximum or minimum capacity of the lungs

• the breath must be maintained during holding and expansion, and past the follow-through to ensure intensity is not lost

• a small exhale just after raising the bow at the target helps to settle the shoulders and body down as the archer comes to the setup position

• meditation training is vitally important for archers to learn breath control

• an archer who is always in control of his breath is an archer completely in control of the entire process of shooting

Breathing helps control the entire process of shooting – everything from nocking the arrow on the string to drawing the bow. Should an archer begin to huff and puff he has lost the calm in his body and his heart is racing out of control in a haphazard attempt to rush blood around the body. Breathing is the basis for the techniques described in "Rhythm," Chapter 14. Correct breathing prepares the body with strength and power for drawing (Chapter 11), and ensures there is excess energy available for expansion (Chapter 17). Breathing is also very important off the shooting line because various techniques learned in meditation training can be used to calm one's nerves, lower a racing heartbeat, and reduce anxiety.

23 String Alignment and Aiming

String alignment, or the position of the string relative to the sight pin as perceived by the archer while at full draw, is an aiming tool for the eyes to match up consistently with the sight pin.

Surprisingly, many recurve archers either ignore string alignment because the string, at full draw, seems too far outside the plane of their sight, or they overdo it and try to align the string through the center of the top and bottom limbs. Recurve archers could learn something from their compound brethren with regards to string alignment by acknowledging its importance, peep or no peep.

Whereas a compound archer will center his sight in the peep, a recurve archer will align his string on the inside edge of the sight pin aperture. For a right-handed archer, the left edge of the string should just touch the right outside edge of the aperture. See figure 23.1 for a series of examples detailing various string alignment.

String alignment should only be checked once the archer has completed holding, after transfer, and has begun the expansion/aiming process. Clearly, if one is making big changes to string alignment, the changes should be made on a blank bale target because string alignment is something that needs to naturally fall into place. Making large changes to head position, anchor position, bow cant, or any other major change of positioning to achieve correct string picture is not conducive to accurate shooting. Before addressing a target, archers must learn their string alignment on blank bale until muscle memory alerts them to any inconsistencies. Once on the range, only slight adjustments will need to be made if the archer has become comfortable with a consistent string alignment.

Correct string alignment   **Wrong side of aperture**   **String too far away from aperture**

FIGURE 23.1

Pay close attention to the subtle differences between each of these examples. Having the string on the incorrect side of the aperture, as shown in the middle example, often creates aiming and expansion difficulties because the string has to cross over the archer's vision of the sight pin. Having the string too far away from the aperture, as seen in the far right example, is most often a result of incorrect head positioning. Nearly all archers need to cant the bow very slightly to the right (for right handed archers) to maintain correct head positioning and achieve proper string alignment (left example).

FIGURE 23.2

Moving string alignment during expansion - Incorrect

Changing string alignment is the number one cause of left and right arrows, especially when the group's height is the size of the gold, but it's width is the size of the red. Take special care to pick a string alignment and do not allow it to change during holding, aiming, and expansion.

FIGURE 23.3

Incorrectly, the sight pin is seen with such clarity, and instead the target is viewed as blurry. In all the other examples within this chapter, notice how the sight pin is viewed as semi-transparent – that is the correct type of focus. The sight should be seen in double, not the target, because the focus is far past it. See figure 23.5 for more details.

While the first important half of string alignment is its position, the second important part is maintaining that position during expansion so it remains dependable. This is not a trivial matter – many archers will check their string alignment right after anchoring but will be unaware of any subsequent changes. Inconsistent string alignment is the number one cause of left and right arrows. If an archer does not maintain consistent string alignment through expansion, precise aiming is negligible. See Figure 23.2 for an example of this phenomenon.

FIGURE 23.4

Here we can clearly see string alignment against the archer's eye. The camera has good alignment with the string and the sight aperture. Notice how the archer is looking on the aperture side of the string, not through the string and the riser. In his vision the string is on his right and sits just beside the aperture.

FIGURE 23.5

The following two pictures finally put to rest the old question about whether to look at the sight or at the target. The concepts here build off figure 23.3, which showed an incorrect focus on the sight pin instead of on the target. In the first picture on the top, the yellow lines represent the archer focusing on the target. Far into the distance, as represented by the bottom of the picture, the images from his left eye and his right eye coincide: the result is a single, clear image that is in focus. He will actually see two sight pins because the lines-of-sight generated by his left and his right eyes are far from converging when they pass over the sight. The sight pin distance is noted on the first picture as the white line. See how the yellow lines intersect the white line at two separate places: this is what causes the dual sight pins. Due to all archers having one dominant eye, there will be a faded, nearly transparent, second sight pin that is generated by the non-dominant eye. Now, looking at the red lines, notice how they intersect as they cross the white line. This means the sight pin will be very clear, in focus, and there will only be one image. However, looking at the bottom of the picture, which represents the target, notice how the red lines touch the edges of the picture in two distinct places, quite far apart. Now, instead of seeing one target, the archer will see two, as shown by the two red lines representing the focal direction of each individual eye.

The second picture shows the same effect, but from the perspective of the archer. In the correct example, the yellow lines represent the correct, target-oriented focus. As the yellow lines cross the plane of the sight pin, notice how again there are two yellow lines, which will result in two sight pins, not two targets. The second, very transparent sight pin is to the right of the more distinct sight pin (and not on the left eye's red line) because should the right eye be closed, the left eye would see the image of the transparent target to the right, in horizontal alignment with the sight pin which, in the picture, is mostly transparent and faint. Were the right eye closed, however, the archer would see only one sight pin, and it would not appear to be transparent or faint.

To avoid any confusion: an archer on the shooting line should only see one target. The second transparent target is drawn in to show what it would look like if the archer were to focus on the sight pin, as represented by the red lines. Though the archer will only see one target, he will see two sight pins. Were the archer to switch his focus to the sight pin, he would see two targets.

Aiming goes hand-in-hand with string alignment. The same type of focus needed to establish and maintain string alignment is needed to use a sight pin while aiming in a controlled and relaxed manner. It is of the utmost importance that the archer only keep his eyes on his aiming point at the target, and never on the sight pin or string themselves. String alignment is done completely with peripheral vision, and the perception of the sight pin is done with parallel vision, or the same type of vision used to see the magic 3-D images. Parallel vision is focusing one's eyes at a divergent point far in the distance (the target), and using secondary vision to notice things at much closer proximity (the sight pin). It is called parallel vision because the sight lines of each eye which views the closer object are nearly parallel when they are focused far in the distance. Shockingly enough, this means the archer should see two sight pins! One is generated by the dominant eye, and one is generated by the non-dominant eye. See figure 23.3 for an example of incorrect eye focus on the sight pin by paying close attention to how the sight pin is bright and has clear edges while the target is blurred and transparent.

FIGURE 23.6

Here we see an example of aiming off, and an example of acceptable pin float. Because the aiming point is about a 9.5 at nine o-clock, or halfway through the nine ring, pin float will drift into the eight ring, no matter how much the archer tries to control it. Even with float like this, all the arrows will go in the gold so long as the wind continues to blow consistently.

Staring at a fixed, unmoving target far in the distance will steady the hand and create the smooth circular flowing and wobbling that is natural for the sight pin. See figure 23.6 for an example of an acceptable amount of pin float. It is not possible to hold the bow noticeably steadier than is shown in the picture, so one should not attempt to do so. While wobbling a normal amount, should the archer become distracted by the wobbling, he has already shifted his focus from the target and onto the sight pin. Eye movement is nearly instantaneous, and can happen too fast for conscious control. Shifting of focus to the sight pin is the biggest culprit of over-aiming, and is a product of an archer's desire to hold the bow ever steadier and more in the center of the target before the string releases. Over-aiming leads to hesitation, incorrect expansion, and, subsequently, poor grouping. Of course, an overall lack of attention to aiming will also not produce good grouping, so it is a delicate balancing act an archer must play.

Aiming off is more a concept of eye focus (Chapter 26) than of aiming. By picking a new aiming point and maintaining eye focus on that location, aiming takes place the same as before, but with the bow pointed in at a new point off-from-center. Aiming off is difficult, because it is very easy to lose focus on an aiming point in the six ring by shifting the eye focus to the gold just at the moment of release. Eye focus must be held on the aiming point through release and follow-through. This becomes especially difficult to do when an archer is aiming off on 'ten-edge' or 'nine point five.' Aiming so precisely involves relatively smaller differences in distances, and thus ever more awareness and control is needed to precisely maintain the chosen aiming point.

Sight apertures without pins can be used for many beginning archers to learn eye focus and aiming, but nearly all top-level archers use a sight aperture with a center pin to give them more precise aiming, especially when aiming off. See Figure 23.7 for a selection of acceptable apertures. Aperture size and color can greatly affect the emotions an archer feels while shooting. Someone who has a precise personality should probably use a larger aperture of muted color so he is not overly distracted by aiming. A large, glowing, red/orange fiber optic is definitely not for everyone. It is surprising how little contrast is needed between the target and the site pin to achieve precise aiming. The more an archer can absorb himself into the target the more he will become still. If an archer is struggling with expansion, try using a less noticeable color (white, grey, black, clear plastic) or remove the pin completely and only shoot with a ring.

FIGURE 23.7

These pictures show acceptable types of apertures for shooting. Notice the differences in color and shape. Size is difficult to show here, however the aperture on the left (the inner ring) is slightly smaller than the other two. Nearly all top archers shoot with an internal dot for precise aiming.

Review

The contradiction inherent to aiming is that concentrating on it creates anxiety and distracts the archer from his primary goal of angular expansion. Precise aiming must be used concurrently with controlled angular expansion to shoot high scores. The contradiction is extremely frustrating to all archers as they are inherently aware of this problem and must fight it with every arrow they shoot. However, to be specific, aiming is a byproduct of body control, not the origin of it. Simply put, the arrow goes where it is pointed. Aiming, then, can only be thought of as an organized and clumped region of various instantaneous points. Continuing, this means that aiming has nothing to do with the center of the target. One can aim at anything, and surely that is where the arrow will go if that is where it is pointed. Thus, aiming in archery specifically deals with pointing arrows in a consistent manner such that they impact the target in a desired pattern – in the center of the target.

The goal of the archer should be to focus not on aiming, but on his body stillness and control, angular expansion, and eye focus at his aiming point, and subsequently aiming will become more precise. Better, more consistent, and more precise aiming cannot be achieved by trying to hold the sight pin steady against the target! This is the difference between process based thought and outcome based thought. When an archer is truly connected with his body and his bow, he aims not just with the bow or the arrow, but with his entire body. His arm does not waver so much as his stomach pushes its energy out through his body to brace against the wind. It is not possible to remain completely still, but one can fight the wind or fight his wavering, or else he can move smoothly and fluidly with them, never panicking that the arrow will land in a less than desirable location.

The key elements to remember about string alignment and aiming are:

• string alignment should sit on the outside edge of the aperture (on the right side for right handed archers and on the left side for left handed archers)

• string alignment position must remain constant during expansion

• both eyes should always be kept open to have the clearest vision of the target, the sight pin, and the string

• one should see two sight pins because his eye focus is on the target, not on his sight

• eye focus must be established on the aiming point desired, allowing the sight pin to float freely around this point

• one can aim just as well in the first second as he can in the third second – do not waste any time attempting to "get ready"

String alignment is largely controlled by head position (Chapter 6). Even very small changes in twist, tilt, or lean of the head can drastically change the string picture at full draw. Sometimes very small amounts of bow cant can be used to achieve the correct string position. The cant should only be done such that the top limb tip moves slightly to the right (for right handed archers). The archer is in a weaker position if the tip leans to the left.

Aiming works in direct conjunction with eye focus (Chapter 26), as eye focus sets the focal point for aiming. The sight pin will float around the focal point on the target established by the archer as the aiming point. If the archer shifts his eye focus to notice how much his sight pin is moving, aiming is undone. Aiming also works with timing (Chapter 24), as timing pertains to how long one aims before the string releases. The general rule of thumb is that the more nervous the archer is, or the more important the competition, the slower his timing will become, and the more out of control he will be. Thus, the archer must focus solely on the angular expansion of the drawing shoulder to smoothly and swiftly expand through the clicker. As his desire grows to hold the bow more and more still, to aim more and more in the middle of the target, his angular expansion diminishes proportionately. Arrow after arrow will become more and more difficult to shoot because each arrow will begin taking far greater amounts of strength and concentration than his practiced arrow. With sudden quickness, an archer can completely lose control and have a meltdown. It is a vicious cycle.

24 Timing

Timing, the little brother of rhythm, is the duration of expansion that allows for a fluid, controlled, beautiful shot.

More so than rhythm, timing is the first thing to break down under pressure. The best archers in the world shoot after holding between one and a half to three seconds, because aiming consistency and focus begin to fall off rapidly after four seconds. Anything less than one second tends to be sloppy and difficult to repeat. There are some archers who have success shooting with timing lasting five seconds or more, however this is very rare and not a teachable method. More important than the duration of timing is the consistency of timing. It is better for an archer to have all of his arrows take between two and a half and three seconds (a six arrow example: 2.5 seconds, 2.75, 2.5, 3, 3, 2.5) than to have some arrows shot smoothly and quickly, but struggle and shoot slowly on others (2.5, 1, 4, 1.5, 3, 4.5 seconds). While it is not important for an archer to shoot with exactly the same timing every arrow, a range of variation between 0.5 second to 1 second is ideal. Shooting with consistent timing is a byproduct of the rhythm and fluidity established earlier in the shot (Chapter 14). Consistent timing allows the archer to focus intently for a short period of time, and frees him from the demand of maintaining such an effort over long durations. Should the clicker go off too fast, it is possible for the archer to be caught off guard and spoil an arrow, because he had not yet mentally and physically prepared his body to shoot. The same can be said if expansion should take longer than the archer would like. There is a window of consistency that encompasses eye focus, holding intensity, aiming, and expansion intensity. Once the archer passes beyond the duration of the window, expanding through the clicker requires extra strength or control he may not have. The extra burst of strength is not something the archer trains for, does not understand how to control, and subsequently has a greater chance of losing the holding balance of the shot.

FIGURE 24.1

Learning to consistently achieve good timing while maintaining control and beauty is like learning to flow while dancing instead of just stepping in the correct pattern. To confidently expand through the clicker without hesitation the body must remain powerful, yet relaxed; focused, yet calm.

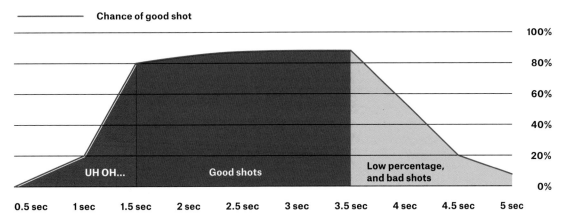

FIGURE 24.2

This graph shows a curve that represents the likelihood of an archer making a good shot based on how many seconds he holds. Not everyone will have a curve that looks like this: some archers are able to consistently hold 1 to 1.5 seconds and are still able to control the shot. Other archers will have a curve that stays flatter, longer. However, the 1.5 to 3.5 second 'good shot' window shown here is standard. The first part of the curve, the 'uh oh' section, does not indicate an archer should wait until 1.5 seconds to begin trying to shoot the arrow. Instead, the chart indicates that should an archer expand through the clicker before he has prepared both his body and his mind, there is a high probability of a poor shot. For most archers, it takes about 1 to 1.5 seconds to calm the mind and body enough to result in a good shot. The flattest part of the curve is in the middle. This is when the body and mind are focused on expansion and are prepared for the string to release. The last part of the graph is the yellow section, which represents the focus cooling down. It is more likely that an arrow held too long will be better than an arrow held not long enough, however, holding too long will warrant a lower percentage shot than the optimum range indicated by the middle of the graph. The brain and eyes can concentrate on a fixed point for around four seconds before concentration begins to fade.

Rushing into expansion with the intent of keeping consistent and fast timing is a mistake frequently made by beginning and advanced archers alike. While success in archery is highly correlated with consistent and fast timing, achieving the holding balance at full draw and controlling the body's intensity is more important than shooting with fast timing. The only way to achieve the desired consistent and fast timing is to establish the holding balance, controlling the body's intensity at full draw. When the body is settled and ready for expansion, only then can consistent power and intensity be used to expand through the clicker. Archers must expand manually, consciously. However, forcing expansion without first controlling intensity will likely cause the archer to resort to finger and hand pressure. Should the fingers squeeze through the clicker, there is a high probability of losing control of the shot. All this can happen despite shooting with fast and consistent timing. The cure for this malady is to take another half second after transfer to secure the holding balance and control the body's intensity. Then, expansion can begin when the archer feels ready. This extra half second is not a pause, it is a continuation of the transfer step with an emphasis on the archer feeling and controlling the shot. This does not make the archer hold for an additional half second, instead, by taking the extra half second to focus on holding, expansion will happen smoother, easier, and more consistently. In most cases, the archer will shoot faster than if he had not taken the extra half second to control the force of his body.

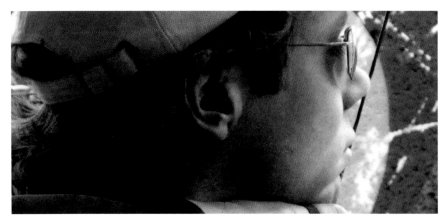

FIGURE 24.3

Shooting with ear plugs can be a good way to center the focus of the body on holding and expanding. The heartbeat becomes easily audible, and can act as an internal metronome to help establish consistency with timing.

Think of it like this: Beginning expansion before controlling body intensity is like pushing a rock up a steep hill. Establishing the holding balance at transfer is like having reached the top of the hill and now the boulder only requires a nudge to get it rolling down the other side. Some archers think they have to scream, "EXPAND!!" in their heads to force themselves to expanding through the clicker. The archer that completes transfer, feels the holding balance, and then begins expanding will only have to whisper, "Ok, now I am ready – go." Archery is a sport of quiet minds.

In the learning process, the best way to keep timing is to count, 1, 2, 3 . . . while at full draw. Once transfer is complete and the holding balance is reached, expansion starts and the archer should begin counting silently in his head. If he reaches a count of five, the archer should let down the bow and start the shot over again. But, do not allow letting down to become a habit. It can ruin the confidence of an archer and should be avoided at all costs. Many archers develop a keen mental awareness of time, however, some top level archers still count out their timing, especially during training. Under pressure, the awareness of time can easily become skewed. To cure this problem, shooting with a metronome can help firmly establish the correct pattern. Eventually, after much practice, archers develop a feel that corresponds to the correct timing. However, in high pressure situations like Olympic Round match-play, timing is still the first technique element to break down.

The greatest remedy for poor timing is simply to shoot more arrows. There is no magic pill to swallow that will alleviate concern about proper execution or forcibly cause an archer to expand through the clicker. The only way to acquire better timing is to shoot, and shoot a lot. Top level archers shoot hundreds of arrows a day, sometimes as many as a thousand in a single day, quickly, smoothly, and with good timing to build up a base of feeling. Years of practice are needed before an archer can maintain good timing under the highest pressure. It is helpful if a coach records the timing of each shot, and computes 6 arrow, 36 arrow, and 144 arrow averages for his archer. These averages can help archers work towards a goal with their timing.

Review

Under pressure, consistent timing is the first thing to break down. Anxiety and fear makes archers aim more, and become more tentative expanding through the clicker. To combat this, archers must concentrate strongly on angular expansion in the drawing shoulder. Repetitions of tens to hundreds of thousands of arrows are needed to build up a base of fast and consistent timing, such that it will remain uniform under pressure. Small things that help with achieving better timing are practicing with a metronome, asking a coach to record arrow timings, or shooting with ear plugs to listen to the heart.

The key elements to remember about timing are:

• the optimal amount of time it should take to shoot the arrow after achieving holding is between 1.5 - 3.5 seconds

• beyond 5 seconds it becomes very difficult to maintain concentration, focus, and control – archers must learn to force themselves to shoot faster

• letting down because timing is too long is a disease and should be avoided as carefully as one would avoid a deathly contagious person – learn to shoot with correct timing

• archers must learn to shoot the arrow with correct timing even if it does not "feel right," because an archer's feeling of comfort will change – do not let down

• strong eye focus will keep the mind concentrated on a fixed object, allowing the body to calmly and quickly expand through the clicker

• one can aim just as well in the first second as he can in the third second – do not waste any time attempting to "get ready"

Timing, eye focus (Chapter 26), and aiming (Chapter 23), saturate the area of the brain that is concerned with where the arrow shall hit. The more the brain can concentrate on strong, smooth, and swift angular expansion, the better. No archer falls outside the laws of timing, as everyone must learn to shoot his shot within 3.5 seconds. With greater skill at hitting the center of the target, an archer must concentrate harder on maintaining good timing. Becoming "careful" is the worst thing that can happen to an archer. It is common to feel rushed, anxious, and out of control. Shoot anyway. The more one practices, the more his anxiety will fade away. See Chapter 28, "The Emotionality of Shooting," for continued talk on this subject.

25 Body Awareness and Control

As archery is a
do sport, or a
martial arts sport,
considerable training
must be undertaken
to learn command
of the body in a
controlled manner.

Body awareness and control is a sense archers develop over time as they learn to hone the forces of the body deep within its core. This gives archers strength and stillness beyond their normal capabilities. There is not a series of steps or processes one must complete to develop and refine body control, so this chapter is more a discussion on how one becomes mindful of the forces of the body.

When one is a beginner learning archery, the positions and postures of the body are all separate entities and events. The head cranes in all directions, the hips twist with a mind of their own, and the shoulders continually fight a losing battle to stay in place as fatigue invariable sets in. While picking up the bow the archer will sway on his feet and lean his hips in all directions. Nothing is connected. Even a gentle breeze is enough to disturb the archer's body and wreak havoc on his technique.

FIGURE 25.1

Here we see an archer who has lost the power from his body's core and is bent forward at the waist. See how the head position attempts to compensate for the imbalance, leaving the archer looking strained and uncomfortable.

FIGURE 25.2

Even as the arrow flies through the air, we can see the archer maintaining complete control of his posture, body positioning, and follow-through. It is control through the shot that will ensure each and every arrow goes into the gold. Power must be held deep in the abdomen to finish the shot like this.

All of these things are perfectly normal. No one is born having perfect body control and awareness. No one is born having a sense for perfect posture. After familiarizing oneself with the complicated motions of archery, the body can begin to settle and relax. This is when body awareness and control become paramount to success. As is detailed in the stance and posture chapters, 1 and 2 respectively, the main intensity of the body must be stored deep within the abdomen, below the line of the waist. When one loses body control it is because his source of intensity is no longer contained within the core and is spreading throughout his body in all directions. Maintaining body control is the state of being mindful that all parts of the body must be connected as one. The strength to hold the powerful force of the bow comes from within the core of the body, not in the extremities with which one holds onto the string or the grip of the bow. Our arms are no more useful than large levers attached to a powerful foundation, and thus must be used in this manner.

FIGURE 25.3

Here we can see an archer who maintains great body control through the moment of execution. There is no visible change in posture, head positioning, or power in these two photos. This desired equal-opposite reaction to the shot is only possible by creating a powerful foundation in the core of the body.

Another critical element to body control is the concept known as efficiency of motion. An archer who is efficient drawing and shooting a bow is an archer who makes as few motions as possible and in the smoothest and most straightforward manner. The fingers should hook the string once, and the head position should be set once. Any motion or movement that is not there for the express purpose of shooting a bow with the utmost care and control is one that does not need to happen. An uncomfortable, out of control archer is one who moves more than necessary.

After learning that all technique elements are connected and that a seemingly benign technique element such as foot balance can affect head position or shoulder alignment, it is time to focus on maintaining control through the execution phase of the shot. If the archer has correctly balanced the forces of his body inside his bow, upon release there will be a harmonious breaking of the torques. It will appear as if the shot pops open. Incorrect forces contained in the body can be noticed immediately in the brief hundredths and tenths of a second after the string has begun to slip through the drawing fingers. The hips may briefly twitch, or the stomach might lose some of its tension. The bow arm may lose its rotation or the top finger may fly open upon release. A reaction especially difficult to control, many archers may experience a brief snapping of the head, seen as a twisting to the side, or a jolting downwards, just as the string is releasing. All of these are symptoms of a loss in body control and the archer must develop an awareness to each of these motions to learn how to control them.

FIGURE 25.4

Clearly these archers are just having fun, but it is
helpful to see an example like this to notice just how
odd shooting posture can look when not balancing over
your feet properly. Leaning is an especially pernicious
difficult problem to solve as full body coordination is
required to address deficiencies. While this archer can
maintain a strong core enough to shoot an arrow this
way, he obviously needs support to not fall over!

FIGURE 25.5

This example shows a common loss of body awareness and control. In the left photo, the archer allowed his bow arm shoulder to slowly elevate upon reaching full draw.

When reminded to press his bow arm shoulder down and out, the same archer achieved the correct position in the second photo.

For example, the reason the bow hand must sit down upon release is because the force of the release hand flying from the string must be balanced with an equal casting of force out the front half of the body. Should the archer not make his bow hand sit, the force of the bow jumps forward, but the body will be unable to compensate. The bow arm will drop because the force of the bow is too great to control. By throwing the bow hand down, directing and controlling the force of the bow, one can keep his bow arm up and finish strongly toward the target. Moreover, by casting force out the front of his body, this will make the back half more controlled and powerful. The energy of the body must be balanced. Should one struggle with the fingers releasing the string, most often the answer is found by looking in the bow arm, hand, or shoulder, not by trying to improve the string release itself. This is the seemingly paradoxical nature of archery.

In the end, archery must look beautiful. Though it is channeling powerful forces, the body must appear calm and composed. The bow must be drawn with the grace of a dancer and held with the strength of the mighty Atlas. Upon release, the archer must appear as though the sudden departure of the arrow is an extension of his body, an effortless loosing of power with the softness of a leaf floating down to land upon a pond of still water. Should the release be vigorous and disjointed, the stillness of the water in the body will be shown as rippling waves of tension.

Review

Archery is ultimately a feeling sport. Even the best coach in the world cannot help an archer who does not learn the feel of his body, the position of his weight or power, and the speed at which he moves. The archer is ultimately his only true source of feedback, as his own body is the only thing over which he actually has any real control. For archery, body awareness and control is defined as standing completely still and only moving exactly what is necessary. For some reason, the brain likes to move three things even though the archer only wants to move just one. An archer's body can lean, twist, change balance, lose connection, or simply not do what he commands. Two good rules of thumb to combat these issues are to one, concentrate on only keeping the head completely still, and the rest of the body will follow suit, and two, attempt to press the center of gravity and the power of the body as low to the ground as possible. The low and compact body is much stronger and resistant to unwanted movement than one where the chest is puffed out. Body awareness and control encompasses every chapter of this book because it pertains to how efficiently one is moving through his motions, and how aware of his motions the archer truly is.

The key elements to remember about body awareness and control are:

• the lower the power and center of gravity of the body the better

• just keep the head still – everything else will remain still too

• even small things, like a mouth that is clenched or tight at full-draw, can affect the control of the shot

• use the ground as a source of stillness and strength for the rest of the body

• upon release, the only thing that should move is the string hand flying back around the neck and the bow jumping out of the bow hand. If posture changes, balance is momentarily disturbed or the head jerks upon release, then one is not shooting with great control

• use breathing as a source of calm to keep the body stationary, only moving exactly what is needed for shooting

Like timing (Chapter 24), body awareness and control is only learned through experience. Feeling will change every time a technique element is changed, and thus greater amounts of practice is needed to build up confidence and precision of body control. Lastly, coaches and video cameras are wonderful tools to use when learning better body awareness and control. Feedback is absolutely essential to achieving greater skill at archery.

Living the Archery Life

Let's just get it out of the way right now. None of you shoot archery for the money. The mass-media and advertising-machine that runs the NFL or the NBA does not exist in its juggernaut form for FITA. There are plenty of jobs that take a lot less talent, hard work, and determination, with half the stress and ten times the pay. Young Olympic hopefuls put careers on hold, travel thousands of miles away from friends and family, and spend 10 hours a day shooting, running, and slowly wearing their bodies down to the point of near failure. Sadly, it is not difficult to paint the dark portrait that some may see.

But the archery life is so much more than all the sacrifices. What other sport allows beginners to stand on the same shooting line as Olympic medalists? The travel opportunities are grand for rarely are competitions less than a few hours drive. Suddenly, before our very eyes, a whole community grows up around us. People come from all tracts of life who are passionate about the thwack/thump/twang of the bowstring and the gradual, but deadly arc of the arrow. Especially for teenagers, the effects of archery can be life-changing. Without even delving into the lessons learned about patience, hard work, and quieting one's mind, the exposure to other cultures, opportunity to make friends from thousands of miles away, and the rare gem of traveling to a world championship, can have a profound broadening of perspective. It is difficult to receive this level of diversity when only participating in small-town intramural sports.

For the chosen few, archery becomes a way of life. Year round training becomes normal. Even if only for a moment, the chance to achieve the unfathomable drives them forward with persistent patience. And when their moment comes and that final arrow strikes the gold, it shall be our cheers that help to remind them that it was all worth it.

Friendships are created from a diverse group of people from all around the world. The experiences the professional archer has are not easily forgotten. Month after month, spending 10 hours a day together creates a true family.

LIVING THE ARCHERY LIFE

26 Eye Focus

Eye focus, or the pinpoint awareness and control of one's eye focal point and movement, is the basis of aiming.

As is outlined in Chapter 23, "String Alignment & Aiming," aiming follows the focal point of the eyes. This means that if one concentrates his eye focus on a left eight, aiming will naturally swim around the left eight, and as long as there is no wind and the sight is correct and his aim is true, the arrow should impact left eight. The goal of aiming and eye focus is not to put arrows in the middle of the target, it is instead to put arrows exactly where the archer wants them.

Correct eye focus is obtainable when the head position is rotated far enough toward the target so the pupil remains in the middle of the eye's range of motion. Eyes have the best clarity and vision when they occupy this medium position. If the archer is only able to turn his head so he is peering out of the corner of his eye, he will not be able to focus as intently.

FIGURE 26.1

The intent gaze of this archer on the target is very apparent in this photo. His face remains calm and relaxed, but it is easily noticeable that his eyes are boring a hole into his aiming point. It has been shown that archers are capable of nearly stopping the incessant scanning of the eye, if only for a few seconds, to focus intently on their target. This is known as the moment of stillness. It is a skill that can be acquired after considerable focus training. An example drill would be simply looking at the corner of a picture and trying to look exactly at the corner of the picture for as long as possible. It is common to be able to do this for only a few seconds. Rest and repeat. Over time it is possible to approach ten seconds of near stillness. Because of this short duration of possible focus, aiming must start after the archer has reached the holding position and is ready to shoot the arrow.

FIGURE 26.2

It can be helpful for eye focus training to shoot at night with the target under a spot light. This training blocks out outside visual distractions and forces the archer to focus intently on the target and his aiming point. After a few evenings of practice it is easy to notice a stronger connection with the target.

Eye focus must begin at the set position (Chapter 8), before raising the bow up to the target. This also means that all aiming-off decisions must be done before establishing eye focus, which consequently occurs before raising the bow. Eye focus must not change until after the follow-through, past the time it takes for the arrow to hit the target. By locking in eye focus, one establishes correct direction at the target. All archers have committed the common mistake of raising the bow toward the target and unconsciously shifted their focus from the target to their sight pin. The direction is and always has been the target, and so the mind must always stay pointed in that direction. Maintaining eye focus will help the archer raise the bow correctly as outlined in Chapter 8 Section 2, "Raising the Bow." Most archers do not concern themselves with the details of how they raise the bow at the target, however this is an oversight on their part. Eye focus is most important while holding and expanding. This even includes blinking, as blinking is defined as a brief momentary lapse of eye and brain control. It is not advised to change aiming points at full draw with perceived small wind changes. Archers cannot accurately judge the wind while at full draw. Attempting to do so would only increase hesitation and create insecurity with the shot. Even a slight change of eye focus from nine-point-five to ten-edge deviates one's focus. It is up to the archer to remain honest and maintain his eye focus with pinpoint control.

Many archers do not understand how to shoot in the wind, continuing to aim at the center of the target even though their arrows experience wind drift. Some archers use a canting method, or leaning the bow, to deal with the wind. Others attempt to compensate for wind drift by using 'English', or throwing the bow forcefully to the side, attempting to push the arrow into the ten as the string releases. Still others move their sights to deal with the wind. These methods are flawed because they are either more difficult than necessary, or are outright inconsistent.

Aiming off is the most effective method for shooting accurately in the wind. Over time archers will learn to judge the wind intensity and pick the correct aiming spot. Upon arriving at the shooting field, veteran archers look for trees or flags that give correct indications of wind intensity and direction. At the shooting line, an archer should pay attention to the wind on his skin and the way it sounds in his ears. With time and practice, archers can become very good at accurately judging new aiming points in the trickiest of winds.

FIGURE 26.3

Do not watch the arrow in flight! Keep the
eye focus on the target!

FIGURE 26.4

This is the aiming off drill suggested in the text. Aim for the blue between the yellow lines, scoring how many arrows out of 50 hit the mark. Try to increase the percentage every time!

A good drill for eye focus and aiming is to purposely pick an aiming point toward the edge of the target. Choose the blue (5 and 6 ring) the height of the gold, draw some lines to outline the new target, and attempt to hit the mark from 70 meters. At first it will feel strange and quite difficult, but with time, the uncomfortable feeling will dissipate. As one begins to master eye focus, he will be able to notice the difference in aiming off between nine-point-five or ten-edge. The closer one gets to aiming at the center of the target, the more challenging consistent eye focus becomes. The archer naturally wants his arrows to go in the middle of the target and thus his eyes get sucked into the middle. This is why a small breeze will cause many people to shoot many right nines and eights. The archer thinks he is aiming at the left nine, but in fact his eye focus is getting sucked into the ten at the moment of release.

Watching the arrow in flight is another way archers break eye focus. This is similar to what is described in the previous paragraph where the archer has his eyes sucked into the middle of the target at the last second, thus changing his aiming point. If one watches the arrow in flight, he is changing his eye focus at the last second, and thus changing the aiming point. It is very important archers do not watch the arrow in flight to the target and instead maintain eye focus for the duration of the arrow's flight. With consistent feeling shots and strong eye focus, the archer does not need visual feedback to know his arrow has scored well.

26 EYE FOCUS

FIGURE 26.5

Through the moment of release, this archer keeps his eyes fixed on his aiming point at the target.

Review

Eye focus is nothing more than the position on the target where the eyes hold their gaze. From far distances, this can be a very difficult task when one is concentrating on the difference between nine-point-five, halfway through the nine, and ten-edge, the outermost edge of the ten-ring. This distance is only a few centimeters, and when viewed from a distance of 70 meters, it is no more than an eye-twitch away. However, with practice, archers learn to fix their eye focus on any point at the target, not allowing their gaze to waver. Various games and drills can be practiced to help an archer with his eye focus, but ultimately it comes down to awareness and honesty. "Was I really looking exactly where I needed to?" is a question all archers should continually ask themselves. Especially while aiming off, it is easy for the eyes to wander towards the middle of the target, as that is the desired outcome. It is also common for archers to watch their arrows while in flight. Both of these problems must be fixed immediately or they form bad habits that are notoriously difficult to break.

The key elements to remember about eye focus are:

• the eyes must remain relaxed to maintain consistent eye focus – sunglasses should be worn in bright conditions to reduce eye strain

• the head must be turned far enough to the target that the eyes are as close to their center position as possible as this is where the eyes are the most efficient

• eye focus must be maintained until after the arrow has hit the target – this means that the archer must maintain his focus on the six ring until after the arrow hits the target, not shift his eye focus to the middle while the arrow is in flight

• never watch the arrow in flight

• shooting with spotlights at night can help archers establish good eye focus with their aiming points as there are no other visual distractions to disturb them

• use the stillness of the target as a source of focus to keep the body and bow arm steady while aiming

As was covered in Chapter 23, "String Alignment & Aiming," the eyes must remain fixed on the target while aiming, not on the sight pin. With strong eye focus, timing (Chapter 24) becomes shorter and more consistent because the archer is not overly concerned with his wobbling aim. Meditation training will help build up the great awareness necessary to realize that one's eye focus has shifted from nine-point-five to ten-edge. Sometimes even the smallest change can make the biggest difference.

27 Putting It All Together

After practicing every aspect of archery and its nuances, archers must look at the greater picture.

This chapter will look back on the previous 26 and identify the concepts that must become unforgettable when the archer is alone holding his bow.

The technical side of archery eventually comes down to four main concepts: fluidity, efficiency of motion, control, and angular motion. A brief discourse on the psychological and emotional side of archery is covered in the next chapter, "The Emotionality of Shooting," but for now the focus will remain on the technical side. Before discussing the main technical concepts, there will be a short checklist of very important technique elements that cannot be missed.

The first technique element to remember is the upwards top finger hook. The top finger creates strength at the holding position and causes the snappiest and most powerful releases. The top finger should touch the string just in front of the first joint, with the main pressure on the bottom half of the finger. The fingernail should point back at the archer's throat and in an upwards direction. This finger position requires a great deal of finger strength. SPT holding drills are the best way to increase this strength.

FIGURE 27.1

Here we can see everything from a good upwards hook, great bow hand positioning, and wonderful alignment as the drawing elbow cannot be seen at all.

FIGURE 27.2

The release is a reaction, not an action. Here we see an archer at the moment of release, her drawing hand still tight against her neck, allowing the release and follow-through to happen naturally.

The second important technique element is the pressure point in the grip of the bow. If the pressure point changes during drawing, holding, or at the moment of release, the forces of the bow will not be directed at the target. Misaligned forces will kick the bow to the side and cause left and right scoring arrows. To maintain the correct pressure point and bow hand positioning, the bow hand thumb must be taut and turned out like a hitchhiker's. These first two elements, the top finger hook and the bow hand pressure point, are the only two places where the archer comes in contact with his bow. All other motions, concepts, and ideas must funnel through these two technique elements because they are the only direct interactions the archer has with his instrument.

The third especially important technique element centers around achieving a concept of holding at the loading position. Archers are so anxious to shoot the arrow their minds often race ahead to the expansion phase, at the expense of a good hold. However, at the loading position, the archer should remember that he must feel 80 to 90 percent ready to shoot the arrow. The archer should slow his drawing motions, control the bow, achieve a good loading position, and softly come to the anchor position. If an archer rushes through the loading position, slamming his hand against his face while anchoring, or attempts to shoot the arrow too quickly, he will not be able to control his force. This archer may sometimes be accurate, however, he will never have a good connection with his bow and will not be able to demonstrate consistent accuracy.

FIGURE 27.3

It takes a great
deal of control and
strength to achieve a
good loading position
where the archer
can take his time to
focus his intensity
on holding and
execution.

Understanding that release is a reaction, and cannot be controlled, is the last technique element to discuss. The mantra that all archers should have permanently etched into their brains is, "Expansion is the first part of the follow-through." This one sentence helps remind the archer of the goal of expansion (to get to the follow-through position), the direction of expansion, and its link to the culmination of the shot. Expansion is the last action the archer is capable of initiating. Therefore, the release and the follow-through are simply reactions from this last action. A better release is not created by trying to keep the hand tighter to the neck or control the fingers from flying open, it is created by expanding correctly through the body, through the neck, and not changing finger pressure prior to release. The correct follow-through position will happen when the correct torque, meaning angular motion and intensity, is used during expansion. Once an archer realizes this last importance on the strength, direction, conviction, and consistency of his expansion, all other things will leave his mind while shooting.

Fluidity is a concept all great archers demonstrably possess. Fluidity is mentioned first out of the main concepts because all great archers, no matter if they shoot the techniques described in this book or not, shoot with an ease that is born of hundreds of thousands of repetitions. Top Korean archers tell of having developed their fluidity by shooting almost 1000 arrows a day, for years during grade school. When the masterful athlete demonstrates profound fluidity in front of a crowd, the sound of applause follows. The applause comes from a deep-seated human understanding about fluidity of motion, an understanding that is greater than ability in even the most practiced athletes, from a crowd who cannot replicate what they have just seen. The masterful athlete spends so much time on the practice range so when he steps up to the line he does not have to think of individual technique elements. Instead, he focuses on the motion and feeling, the synchronization of the tiny steps blending into one. It is possible to quickly learn one element of a professional athlete's repertoire, but to incorporate all of the difficult steps into one motion takes fluidity and control. This concept of fluidity, or one motion, does not mean that changes of direction, power, speed, or intensity do not occur, but instead means fluidity encompasses all of the motions and preserves their concepts, rounding the edges so each step blends seamlessly into the one after it.

FIGURE 27.4

A fluid shot is a must for maintaining control and consistency under pressure.

A fluid archer will have no breaks or pauses between when he first hooks the string until after the arrow hits the target. It is possible to still talk about the setup position, something that is learned as a static position, but instead of a full-stop occurring, a fluid archer would change the speed of his motions when nearing this position, take the extra care to position his body just so, and smoothly continue drawing the bow. It can be thought of as pouring a glass of water, sometimes in a bigger stream, and sometimes not, but never allowing the stream to become individual water droplets. This is how one must draw and shoot a bow. This concept requires conviction to execute because once the shot has started, it must continue without break until it is finished. An archer must smoothly and confidently raise his bow at the target, never hesitating or pausing to recheck himself. The fluid archer trusts his aim and shoots to make his technique look beautiful, not even caring where the arrow lands. While possessing fluidity means the archer does not stop or pause, it also means he does not suddenly change speeds, nor does he use any jerky motions. Beginners commonly jerk the bow up at the target, or jerk the string back to their faces, come up to anchor from the loading position too quickly, or jam their shoulders around trying to expand through the

FIGURE 27.5

The efficient archer does not waste any motions in drawing and shooting the bow.

FIGURE 27.6

Control means the archer only shoots when he wishes. A good drill for learning control is to draw back at a mirror, expand through the clicker, hold for an additional three seconds, and let down.

clicker. If a change of speed or direction is necessary, as when the archer raises the bow above the target and begins starting the drawing motion, it is the transition between raising the bow and beginning to draw that will distinguish a fluid archer from a choppy one. The fluid archer will use the stillness of his body to control his motions, rounding the upward motion into the drawing motion, and will accelerate the bow first up and then slow it down. He will transition into the drawing motion slowly, but pick up speed as the string comes back towards his face. Then he will again round out the long and powerful drawing motion, containing the forces generated in his back muscles so he can smoothly and confidently reach the loading position, and again transition with increasing slowness up to the anchor position, and eventually all the way to holding, where he is now able to begin execution.

The second main concept, efficiency of motion, stems from fluidity. These concepts are corollaries – by their very definition they seem to imply the other. Both are so essential and important to beautiful shooting that they each deserve separate attention. Efficiency of motion is nothing more than brevity and concision of motion. Essentially, efficiency of motion is not moving anything more than exactly what is needed, and only doing so in the most straightforward manner. Fluidity, which is the blending of individual steps into the smoothest routine, reaches another level of precision when it is blended with efficiency of motion. Efficiency of motion dictates that the archer should move as little as possible. This means no extra fidgets, no extra adjustments, and no up-and-over motions when the diagonal is the shortest distance. At first, it may be physically easier to lift and then twist, but with enough practice the two motions can be blended together until they become one motion. It should look surprising how little the archer moves, even from when he is first loading an arrow or starting to hook the string. Do not check the hook twice when it is possible to get a good hook on the first try. Do not hook the string and then cock the wrist outwards when it is possible to hook the string with a bent wrist from the beginning. It is easiest to understand this concept when one tries to shoot a bow with the correct technique, but with the caveat of moving as little as possible. There must be no wasted motions or wasted thoughts. Each motion must be directly related to shooting the arrow. This is efficiency of motion. When blended with fluidity, these two concepts come together when trying to shoot with correct technique while moving as little as possible, and doing so as gracefully and fluidly as possible. Great athletes of other sports, along with great Korean archers, practice so much because they understand this level of fluidity and efficiency only comes about through thousands of repetitions.

Control, the third main concept, is the archer's ability to move as efficiently and fluidly as possible, but with pinpoint precision. Control is the archer's ability to move, or to not move, every part of his body, exactly when he wants to – even under stress, pressure, or weakness. It takes control to achieve a good loading position: the archer must contain the powerful drawing forces, storing and directing them inside his body so as to maintain perfect posture, balance, and holding. Control means the archer does not rush what he does not want to rush. Indeed, control takes a great deal of strength. An archer with great control can hold a bow 10-15 pounds (5-7 kilograms) greater than his competition setup for 30 seconds without shaking or feeling strain, then rest for 1 minute and repeat the same 30 second holding, and repeat after a 1 minute rest for a total of 30 minutes or more. Truly, control is much more than strength, as this entire drill must be done without breaks in technique. The top finger hook must be perfect, the bow arm shoulder must stay down, and the alignment must not collapse. To achieve this level of control takes a great deal of practice, intensive training, and patience.

FIGURE 27.7

In an efficient shot routine, every motion
has a reason and blends together
seamlessly.

27 PUTTING IT ALL TOGETHER

FIGURE 27.8

Using angular motion is the only way to consistently
control the powerful force of the bow.

Lastly, the most important element of shooting, the use of angular motion encompasses the previous three main elements of shooting and gives them direction, meaning, and stability. To understand the importance of angular motion, realize that there is no single element of the shooting process that does not involve using angular motions to prepare the body for drawing the bow. An archer must not pull the bowstring back to his face in a straight line. Rather, he should angularly draw the arrow around an imaginary center that runs down his head and spine, transcribing a circular path with his motions. The structure of an archer's shoulder defines its base movement as rotational. To draw in a straight line is not biomechanically sound. Drawing with an angular, or circular motion, is to draw in the way the body is designed. Because the archer is drawing in an angular motion, he shifts his body and exertions such that they are between the riser and the string. Coaches like to say this places the archer "inside the bow." Being "inside the bow" is a stronger position for the body than to be "outside" it, where a linear drawing method would place him. Being outside the bow requires more strength, and control is more difficult.

Biomechanically, bringing the power of the bow closer to the center of the body will allow the archer to better balance and stabilize himself. The only way to bring the power of the bow that close to the center of power within the body is to turn the body inside itself! Turn, an angular word, is the action the drawing shoulder must continually do. At no point should the drawing shoulder not be under angular movement. A reminder about expansion, already priorly discussed, is that the correct angular expansion is actually through the body. When the body is at the holding position, as shown in Chapter 10, "Angular Motion," the string and draw hand must move into and through the neck to continue angular motion. Lastly, these angular motions must be fluid, efficient, and carried out with great control. This is the physicality of archery.

28 The Emotionality of Shooting

_____

When it comes down to it, archery is not a test of man's physical prowess, it is a test of man's heart.

Before we even talk about the stress of shooting in front of thousands of people for an Olympic medal, we need to start at the beginning of archery's test against the soul. It is within man's power to attain victory or defeat: to display courage or cowardice.

When one first picks up a bow and attempts to hit a mark, his physical skill is not adequate to create much anxiety. After considerable practice the archer begins to expect a certain level of performance from his physical skill. Suddenly, he cares. His willful will predominates his thoughts. Whether it is a determination to shoot well or beautifully for others, or more simply, to beat a personal best and improve his confidence, it is now the archer's desire to shoot well that is his limiting factor. Physically, for one arrow, he is capable of shooting near the exact center of the target. For one arrow he is capable of drawing a bow with more grace than Apollo could command. For one arrow, almost anyone can achieve excellence. However, when that one arrow must be repeated with another, and another, on command, the archer begins to question his ability to sustain beauty.

In its simplest form, archery is a task of conquering demons. Indeed, in all sports, and, for that matter, any passion, one must learn the art of controlling the swells of the heart to achieve virtuoso status. In archery in particular, its repetition and protraction makes the continual battle the athlete must fight with his heart unlike that of any other sport. When an archer stands waiting to begin his gold medal match, he merely walks to the line when the buzzer sounds. Adrenaline only make his hands shake more, and thus he avoids any thoughts that would take him down such a path. Excitement is his enemy. In the moment where he experiences the great fight or flight instinct, he must do neither. He must stand in place, gently and carefully draw back his bow, and launch an arrow into the winds. Moreover, in a head-to-head match, each arrow means something different. It is true that the first arrows score the same as the last, but as possible chances of pulling ahead of his opponent dwindle, or the closer he gets to shooting the arrow that sets a world record, the more the archer's heart swells. The more his heart cares. When the desired intangible comes into view, the last arrow to win the match feels immeasurably harder than the first few easy tens. Because always, the heart knows the calculus involved, and seemingly a miscalculated heartbeat can spell defeat should the arrow land millimeters away from his dreams. The moment the archer shoots from a place of need, "I need to make a good shot on this last arrow to win," he has spelled doom for himself. Is it not true that he needed the first arrows just as much?

Just prior to a major competition, nearly every archer sits alone, speaking to no one, internalizing his thoughts and his mind. Archery is a sport of calm.

28 THE EMOTIONALITY OF SHOOTING

The simple truth is that great strength resides in the act of shooting. The archer who shoots to make his physical expression beautiful is very different from the archer who shoots to hit the center of the target. Ultimately, there is greater happiness to be found in shooting for the beauty of expression than for the sake of hitting a mark. Modern psychology talks about the differences between process-based and outcome-based thought. Process-based thought focuses on the actions that will produce a result. Outcome based thought focuses on the result, using excitement and desire to create performance. While all claims about either method are subjective, some logic exists that would argue outcome based thought creates unrealistic expectations and no path towards them. The archer focused on the process is the one who shoots for beauty. He focuses on the details of his motions, smoothing and blending them together until it is not possible to tell where his arms end or the bow begins. The other archer – the outcome archer – pulls the bow back to his face, shaking with the effort and the anxiety of achieving perfection. The bow is not part of him. It is just an instrument that sometimes does his bidding. He is the archer who is neither rooted into the ground, nor walks freely in the heavens above. He hangs between, forever dreading the snap of the bowstring that will tear him in two.

Fear drives all of the failures in archery. What if something, at the crucial moment, goes wrong? A good question, yes, but the correct answer hints at so much more. Something is always going wrong, isn't it? If you have to feel comfortable to shoot the arrow, you are already lost. This answer looks at the desired outcome – a ten on the last arrow of the Olympics to win a gold medal – and reminds all archers that no matter what their goals are, things will never be absolutely perfect while reaching those dreams. Only a fool would ask favors of the wind. Fear drives the heart and mind to demand the impossible – the wind gust that pushes a mistake into the middle of the target. It is the nuances of each moment that makes life alive and real. The archer who shoots the arrow for the beauty of his motions is one within himself, coexisting with the wind, the bees buzzing around his head, and the pitter-patter beat of his excited heart. The illusion of comfort can be so great as to drive the perfectionist mad when he realizes he is very much uncomfortable, and hopelessly out of control. The key to success in these moments is action. Hesitancy is the mind's desire for control, a slowing of action; a prevention of forward thought and motion. The shot practiced endlessly during training is one of smooth, fluid, ongoing motion. However, when the archer stands facing his target, there are no respites from contemplation. Despite feelings of dread, a lack of comfort, and a fear of both success and failure, the only thing the archer can do is shoot his arrow. And in so doing, he must shoot his arrow as he has practiced it a thousand times: unthinking, strong and confident, a true expression of his heart.

Total Archery
Inside the Archer

————————

KiSik Lee
Tyler Benner

3rd edition

Designer: Petr Duba
Editor: Spencer Adamson
Technical Editor: Kurt Eggerling
Cover photography: Bradford Benner

ISBN 13 – 978-0-9824265-3-1
ISBN 10 – 0-9824265-3-4

Astra Archery
2127 Olympic Parkway
Suite 1006 #158
Chula Vista, CA 91915

www.AstraArchery.com